University of Rhode Island Library

The Greek and Macedonian Art of War

THE GREEK AND MACEDONIAN
ART OF WAR

BY F. E. ADCOCK

UNIVERSITY OF CALIFORNIA PRESS.
Berkeley, Los Angeles, London

University of California Press
Berkeley and Los Angeles
California

University of California Press, Ltd.
London, England

© 1957 by
The Regents of the University of California

Fourth Printing, 1974
ISBN: 0–520–00005–6

Library of Congress Catalogue Card No. 57–10495

PREFACE

In THESE lectures which I have been privileged to give on the Sather Foundation of the University of California an attempt is made to describe the art of war as practised by the Greeks and Macedonians. The details of military equipment and of the topographical setting and incidents of particular battles, which have been fruitfully studied by eminent scholars, are here described only in so far as is necessary to explain the factors with which the art of war operated or to illustrate its operation. In dealing with the evidence I have sought to extract what appeared to be most significant for my theme.

Any student of these matters will realize the debt he must owe to the pioneer systematic work of H. Droysen and A. Bauer, as also to the writings of J. Kromayer and G. Veith together with their collaborators in *Antike Schlachtfelder* and in *Heerwesen und Kriegführung der Griechen und Römer,* and, in particular for Alexander and the Hellenistic Age, to the writings of Sir William Tarn. A general acknowledgment is also due to the forceful doctrine of H. Delbrück in his *Geschichte der Kriegskunst* which most nearly approaches the theme of these lectures. Though I have not been able at all points to accept his conclusions, I have profited greatly from his originality and his realistic grasp of the whole art of war.

In the writing of these lectures I have profited from discussions with my friend Mr. G. T. Griffith, who has also been kind enough to read a proof of the book, to its great advantage. For such errors of fact or doctrine as may remain in these pages, I must accept full responsibility. The footnotes are chiefly intended to indicate the ancient evidence, but I have sought to make due acknowledgement to the ideas and conclusions which I owe to modern scholars.

In a more general sense I have been greatly helped by the friendly encouragement of the members of the Department of Classics at Berkeley and especially of its Acting Chairman, Professor Fontenrose. Dr. W. H. Alexander and Mr. H. A. Small, of the University Press, together with the Special Committee for the Sather Lectures, have been most sympathetic and wise counsellors in all matters concerned with the publication of these lectures, and my very best thanks are also due for the care and skill of the staff of the Press.

Finally, I would be very glad to think that the happiness I enjoyed during my stay in this hospitable University has been, in a measure, repaid by whatever value within its chosen field these Sather Lectures may seem to possess.

F. E. A.

CONTENTS

I

The City-State at War

THE MAIN theme of these lectures is how the Greeks and Macedonians applied their minds to the art of war. This does not make the conduct of war a science, which it is not, even today, when machines count for so much. And in antiquity it was the creation, above all, of *human* skill and courage and fortitude. The famous dictum that war is a passionate drama[1] places it in the field of art: it is not scientific in the sense that it is impersonal and dispassionate.

It is tempting to look a trifle askance at war. No one would assert that war is the ideal way of settling disputes. No one would deny that it is the unhappy interruption of the blessings of peace. Of this the Greeks, for example, were very conscious, as they were conscious that it is better to be well than to be ill. But war claimed a place in their lives, whether they wished it to do so or not. And to understand the past it is necessary to study what happened and why, so far as one can. Thucydides said that war is a violent preceptor,[2] and he was thinking that it taught some things that were evil; but war is part of the experience of mankind, and it would be unwise to leave it unstudied, though there are other things that have a higher claim on our attention. So much for my title except that I may add, in passing, that the words "Greek and Macedonian" are not meant to deny the strong possibility that a Macedonian was ethnically a kind of Greek.

[1] Jomini, *Résumé stratégique*, p 30.
[2] Thuc. III, 82, 2.

This first lecture is concerned with the kind of warfare that was characteristic of the historical Greek city-state and of the Greek as a city-state animal, which is what Aristotle called him.[•] Greeks had been at war before their historical age began. There were brave men before Agamemnon, and after him too. The theme of the Epic—the unforgotten common heritage of the Greeks—was "the glorious deeds of men." That is what the blind bard sang of in the hall of Alcinous in Phaeacia.[•] Thus in the *Iliad* hero after hero has his great moment, his *aristeia,* in which his single prowess stands out clear. Each lives before us as he lived to the Greeks who listened to the rhapsode's recital. The stubborn Ajax is stubborn against men and gods. Diomedes has a passionate, youthful masterfulness. Hector, until his doom overtakes him, is the cause of his people personified. The greatest moment of Achilles is that moment when, as the Greeks are being driven back after the death of Patroclus, he stands unarmed at the Trench, and the sound of his sole voice strikes fear into the ranks of Troy. Whatever the old wise Nestor might say of the ranging of armies, by tribes and brotherhoods, the battle of the Epic is, above all, of hero against hero.

All this the historical Greeks remembered as derived from their Heroic Age. But the Epic tradition did not provide them with an art of war; it provided them with a panorama of protagonists. In their own day war had become something far different: it meant the uniting of the armed men of the community to fight shoulder to shoulder, with an orderly, integrated valour. When this is achieved, a true art of war becomes discernible. Just how it was achieved in the dim centuries that lie between Heroic and historical Greece we cannot tell. But we can see, as Aristotle saw, that it is in part a cause, and in part an effect, of the political development of the city-state.

[•] *Politics* I, 1, 9, 1253a.
[•] Odyssey VIII, 73.

We may, for the time being, disregard those few parts of Greece Proper which had not become organized as city-states. Their political life was different, and their way of conducting war was different too. What we are concerned with now is the characteristic political form of the Greeks and its characteristic method of waging war. This was to place in the field as its one dominant arm a phalanx of hoplites. I use phalanx as a convenient word to describe a body of infantry drawn up in close order in several ranks which are also close together.[5]

Hoplites are troops who take their name from their shields. This is as it should be; the character and use of their shields were of the essence of their fighting in battle. The shield was round, rather more than three feet across. It was carried on the left arm, which passed through a ring to a grip held in the left hand. The monuments show that it had become the standard infantry shield of the Greeks before the middle of the seventh century B.C. It covered most of a man's body and it left the right arm free to wield a stout thrusting spear some seven or eight feet long. A hoplite carried a short sword as well, but his spear was his chief weapon. His head was protected by a metal helmet, and he wore a corslet as a second line of defence, and greaves to guard his legs. Such was the hoplite as he stands before us in literature and art.[6]

The hoplite's shield most effectively covers his left side. His right side can gain some lateral protection from the shield of his neighbour on his right. Thus the line of hoplites is the alternation of the defensive shield and the attacking spear, with which each man strikes, usually overarm, in an orderly and yet skilful way. This skill is acquired by early training with perhaps some practice—the evidence for this is slight—when occasion

---

[5] The word was first generally applied to the famous Macedonian phalanx, which was a variant of the hoplite formation with special characteristics of its own. See below, pp. 26 ff.

[6] H. L. Lorimer, "The Hoplite Phalanx," *Ann. Brit. School at Athens*, XLII, 1947, pp. 76 ff.

serves. It is hard to conceive of a method of warfare that, in peace, made a more limited call on the time and effort of most citizens of most communities.[7] When war came it meant a great effort but a rare one, for, in early times, the evidence suggests that wars and battles were not the constant occupation or pre-occupation of the Greeks. They had many other things to do than fight, though when they had to fight they fought well.

The effectiveness of the phalanx depends in part on skill in fighting by those in the front rank, and in part on the physical and moral support of the lines behind them. The two opposing phalanxes meet each other with clash of shield on shield and blow of spear against spear. Their momentum is increased by the impetus of the charge that precedes their meeting. If the first clash is not decisive by the superior weight and thrust of the one phalanx over the other, the fighting goes on. The later ranks supply fighters as those before them fall. At last one side gains the upper hand. Then the other phalanx breaks and takes to flight and the battle is won and lost.[8]

The continuity of the line while the fighting is going on is all-important, and every man in the line knows that his life depends on his neighbour's fighting as steadily, as skilfully, and as bravely as himself. No form of combat could so plainly exhibit the community solidarity that was of the essence of the Greek city-state. It was not the place for single-handed exploits, for the Epic *aristeia* of champions. The desire for personal distinction must be subordinate: it must find its satisfaction elsewhere, as in the great athletic festivals, where men won honour before all

---

[7] Some Greek city-states kept comparatively small formations of picked troops in constant training and readiness. See Pauly-Wissowa, *Realenc.* s.v. Kriegskunst, col. 1831, for details; also (for Argos) *Cambridge Ancient History* (*C.A.H.*) V, p. 258, and, for possible peacetime uses of these troops, Aeneas Tacticus XVI, 7, with Hunter's note *ad loc.* (pp. 151 f.).

[8] The early hoplite army did not, in battle, rely upon the moral and material support of a fortified camp which is so prominent in Roman warfare. We are not well informed for the fourth century. A work on the subject by Aeneas Tacticus has not survived. See further, p. 61, n. 47.

the Greeks. After the battle, each man may recall how well he fought and remind his neighbours that he did, but, in battle, he does not fight alone or for his own hand.

Not all the able-bodied men in the city-state fought in the hoplite phalanx, even though numbers told so heavily in its battles. The city-states had developed as aristocracies, and the nobles would naturally fight, presumably in the front rank, so long as they were young enough to take the field. But more men than these were needed, and the duty and privilege of fighting as hoplites were extended to the members of the middle class who could provide themselves with the necessary equipment. These were at Athens the Zeugitae, which probably means the men who could fight in a rank or file.[9] But at this point in the social order recruitment and the extension of privilege ended. It did not suit the ideas of an early aristocracy to provide equipment for men who could not afford to provide it for themselves, or to train such men to fight on an equality with their betters. Political privilege and the limit of military obligation justified each other. The citizen who did not belong to what was called "those who provide their own shields" might be called on to do some fighting of a kind, but, as will be seen, it was, at this time, of slight value.

Thus the hoplite army was the army of the upper and middle classes, and of these alone, and on this army depended the safety of the community.

Such was the tradition that was established at least as early as the seventh century. It continued with the conservatism that has often made armies the "temples of ancestor worship."[10] The very character of hoplite fighting tended to limit the advance of the art of war. For example, hoplites could fight as a sizable phalanx only where the evenness of the ground allowed close

---

[9] C. Cichorius, "Zu den Namen der attischen Steuerklassen," *Griechische Studien H. Lipsius dargebracht*, pp. 135 ff.

[10] B. H. Liddell Hart, *Elements of War*, p. 131

alignment to be preserved. Herodotus makes the Persian general Mardonius say to King Xerxes, "The Greeks seek out their fairest and smoothest piece of ground and go down to it and fight."[11] The advantage of fighting downhill was so great—for it added to the momentum of the phalanx—that no army could allow its opponent to fight at this advantage. So it would usually be level ground. And in the economy of any ordinary city-state the "fairest and smoothest" ground was the fertile ground that was the most worth fighting to defend.[12] If the enemy could not be challenged on this ground with a fair chance of victory, it was idle to challenge him at all.

This fact set a limit to strategy; as the general character of the hoplite battle set a limit to tactics. For example, if a state is invaded, it is an advantage to offer battle as near to the shelter of its city walls as possible, for that will reduce losses in the event of defeat. But this strategy cannot be adopted if it means yielding to the enemy the control of the state's good land. To defend that land the army of the invaded state must advance to meet the enemy. This means that a strategist can hardly achieve more than bring on a battle on a piece of level ground that suits best the size of his army. Further, as numbers count for so much, it is dangerous to detach forces to gain some strategical advantage; for if the main battle is lost, all is lost with it. The armament on both sides is so similar that superiority in weapons cannot be contrived. In tactics, once battle is joined, a general can hardly control events. In most Greek armies the most that a general can do is to dispose his troops as well as he can, encourage them to fight well,[13] and then fight well himself, as one hoplite among the rest. Napoleon himself could not have altered the course of most hoplite battles once they had begun.

[11] Herod. VII, 9.

[12] See G. B. Grundy, *Thucydides and the History of His Age*, I², pp. 246 ff.

[13] See O. Luschnat, "Die Feldherrnreden im Geschichtswerk des Thukydides," *Philologus*, Suppl. XXXIV, 2, 1942. One of the lost books of Aeneas Tacticus was on the making of speeches by generals.

This does not mean that some generals were not better than others. As will be seen later, a general may take decisions for which high qualities are required. But it does mean there was little inducement to study and advance the art of war. What is called nowadays *logistics,* the ordered supply and moving of troops, was hardly a problem, except when an unusually large army was concerned, as before the battle of Plataea. There was no place for that comparatively modern phenomenon, a general staff, which, in peace as well as war, studies the military problems of a state in any foreseeable conditions. Great experience in command was rare. I have read somewhere that a lady asked one of Wellington's generals how he learnt fighting, and he replied, "How? ma'am, how? By fighting and a deuced lot of it." This salutary education did not come the way of many city-state generals. Further, campaigns were brief.[14] The armies, operating in the summer, wished to be home again for the harvest and the gathering of the grapes and olives. And one battle nearly always settled the business.

The losses of a defeated army were almost invariably greater than those of the victors, even though pursuit, after the hard exertion of the combat, was not prolonged. It was very rare for a defeated army to try its luck again, and, in general, states had no reserve forces, for it had been all-important to be as strong as possible for the first combat. It was the convention for the vanquished to admit defeat by sending heralds to ask leave to collect their dead for burial. The battle was, as it were, a "mass duel,"[15] a trial of strength; and the verdict of the trial was accepted. It would have seemed to the Greeks of this age folly not to know when you were beaten. The victor was appeased or, if he was not, he was left to take the profit of his victory. And through armistice and negotiations a peace was often reached. Greek

[14] Grundy, *op. cit.* I², pp. 249, 257.
[15] W. Rüstow–H. Köchly, *Geschichte des griechischen Kriegswesens von der ältesten Zeit bis auf Pyrrhos,* p. 145; *C.A.H.* IV, p. 166.

states did not, in general, seek the utter destruction of each other by war conducted *à outrance*. Nor did they wish to press matters to the arduous task of besieging the enemy city. And so states passed from war to peace as easily, or more easily, than from peace to war.

But before I leave the battle I should say that there was one Greek army—namely, the Spartan army—that for three centuries at least was preëminent in the field, and that because of the greater training of the men, and their capacity for manoeuvre due to the subdivision and control of their tactical units.[16] In most Greek states the chain of command from general to hoplite was weak: there was no regular officer class,[17] nor was there, what was perhaps more important, a cadre of professional non-commissioned officers, such as the centurions provided in the Roman army. Thus, even if there was scope for manoeuvre there was little power of using it. The Spartan army was capable of manoeuvre within certain limits. This is most clearly seen in its exploitation of an ingrained habit among Greek troops. Thucydides observed how advancing troops tended to edge out towards their right,[18] their unshielded side. They had an instinctive desire to feel themselves more protected by the shields of their right-hand neighbours. Thus the right wing of a hoplite phalanx was apt to some degree to outflank the enemy's left wing. The Spartans exploited this tendency by being able after outflanking their enemy's left to wheel round and roll up the enemy line. This was the more possible because the Spartans advanced, as Milton says, "to flutes and soft recorders" rather than charged at speed. Their disciplined steadiness was not borne down by the impact of the enemy charge, their skill in front-line fighting compensated for its lack of momentum. The united thrust of the line pinned down the enemy until the

[16] Thuc. V, 68, 3.
[17] A. W. Gomme, *Historical Commentary on Thucydides, Book I*, pp. 14, 22.
[18] Thuc. V, 71, 1.

turning movement decided the day. Victory was at home among the red coats of the Spartans, and the spirited Mantitheus in a speech of the orator Lysias pronounces it a truism that everyone knew how dangerous it was to face Spartans in the field.[19]

Such, then, was the hoplite battle—a vehement, concerted effort, short and sharp, for which every man must nerve himself and screw his courage to the sticking point.

This being so, how did war appear to the Greeks' sharp, realistic, and sensitive minds? We see on vases the Greek hoplite preparing to go out to war, spruce with his helmet and with the shield his wife has been polishing—for it may have got blackened as it hung in the chimney corner during months or years of peace.[20] What did he and his fellows think of it all? In the Epic, behind the brightness of heroic exploits, there is now and then a strong sense of the tragedy of war, the cost of these exploits. And throughout the poetry of the classical age this note is often heard.[21] "Sweet is war," writes Pindar,[22] "to him who knows it not, but to those who have made trial of it, it is a thing of fear." In the *Agamemnon*[23] there is an elegiac tone about the men who have died before Troy, and the herald's story of victory is not all exultation. Euripides in the *Troades* has harsher words for that same victory. I can remember no phrase more poignant than Pericles' words of the young men who had perished in Samos: "It was as if the spring had been taken from the year."

To respond to the call to fight for the city was a plain duty that admitted of no hesitation. But it was, to the Greeks, a hard duty—the interruption of their happy lives, the risk of passing

---

[19] Lysias XVI, 17.

[20] Aristophanes, *Acharn.* 279.

[21] W. E. Caldwell, *Hellenic Conceptions of Peace;* A. W. Gomme, *Essays in Greek History and Literature*, pp. 122 ff.; W. Nestle, "Der Friedensgedanke in der antiken Welt," *Philologus*, Suppl. XXXI, 1, 1938.

[22] Frag. 120 (Turyn), vv. 5 f.

[23] E.g. vv. 445–462.

from the warm company of men to the chill shades of death. And they knew that bravery, highly as they prized it, is not an everyday possession. The Spaniards have been among the most valiant of soldiers, but they have a significant saying—"he was a brave man *that day*."[24] And to the Greeks war was not an everyday business. Their courage—except for that of the Spartans—was not a cool steadiness born of ingrained, rigorous discipline that shuts the mind to fear. It has been said, with much truth, that the main difference between the Greek and the Roman art of war lay in the fact that the Greeks in general had not, by instinct or training, the discipline that was the chief ingredient in Roman soldiership.[25] Thus what best suited the Greek citizen-soldier was a form of battle in which the intensity of one short effort carried him forward, in which a man's duty to his immediate comrade was the best spur to his intent. It was not a needless parade when generals, at the eleventh hour, addressed their troops to hearten them and give them the belief in victory that was half the battle. And it was to warm their hearts for the decisive clash that most Greek armies shouted as they charged, so that each man might borrow from the general stock of courage and confidence. If the day went against them, if they were thrust back in what the poet called "the turn of the spear," Greek hoplites would often break and run, resisting, if they could, the temptation to jettison their shields with the *insouciance* of the poet Archilochus:

> My shield I left beside a bush, because I must.
> It's not the poor thing's fault— Some Saian now
> Has joy of it, but I have saved my life.
> What care I for that shield? A parting curse on it.
> Another day I'll buy one, just as good.[26]

---

[24] Quoted by Jomini, *Précis de l'art de la guerre*, p. 617.

[25] J Kromayer–G. Veith, *Heerwesen und Kriegführung der Griechen und Römer*, pp. 1 f., citing Delbrück.

[26] Frag. 6 Diehl[3].

The very liveliness of the Greek mind made panics—which, Thucydides says, are apt to befall great armies"—one of the chances of war. The readiness to admit defeat was the other side of the vehement *élan* which Greek armies so often manifested. By contrast, when Alcibiades in the *Symposium*[28] is praising Socrates, he tells how, when the Athenian army was routed at Delium, Socrates "stalked along, regarding friend and enemy composedly, so that everyone could tell from far away, that if one attacks this man, he will repel him with stout courage. And so he came off safe with his companion."

Thus far I have limited myself to the battle between hoplite phalanxes because it was such battles that occur where Greek meets Greek in the period with which we are concerned. It is seldom that hoplites had to fight against other kinds of troops. Cavalry is rare, and its effect is limited for reasons I will give in a later lecture. So far as the decisive battle is between hoplites, light-armed troops are at a discount in citizen armies. They are most effective where they are most at home, viz., in communities in which the social order or the terrain does not naturally lend itself to hoplites and hoplite fighting. But with such communities and such terrains we are not here concerned.

It may seem a strange way of beginning a study of the art of war to argue that for so long there was so little scope for it. But even when strategy and tactics are, as it were, conventional in wars between Greeks, it may be otherwise when new enemies with new methods of warfare force themselves on the attention of the city-states. And this the Persians did in the two enterprises that led to the battle of Marathon and then eleven years later, to the battle of Plataea. The Persians had conquered from Iran to the Levant by the skill of their cavalry and archers,[29] and this

[27] IV, 125, 1; cf. Aeneas Tacticus XXVII.
[28] 221A–B.
[29] W. W. How, "Arms, Tactics and Strategy in the Persian War," *Journ. Hell. Stud.* XLIII, 1923, pp. 117 ff.

fact presented to Greek generals a problem which had to be solved if Greek freedom was to be preserved. The problem was to find a time and a place in which hoplites could win the day. It appears beyond doubt that the Athenian general Miltiades could claim high credit for the victory of Marathon, not so much for his conduct of the battle as for his discernment that a moment had come when, for whatever reasons, he could take the Persians at a disadvantage, when he could launch a decisive attack in which the weight and thrust of his hoplites came into their own.

And the same is true of the Spartan general Pausanias at the battle of Plataea. He had been set a strategical problem which, with his composite army, was beyond his power to solve.[30] But to him too there came a moment when, if he seized it aright, he could turn the probability of defeat into the certainty of victory. His patient, disciplined Spartans and their comrades in war, the men of Tegea, had endured the rain of arrows unflinchingly until the Persians were so massed together that they were within the reach of a deadly attack. And Pausanias showed the sense of timing which has been the gift of the ablest captains. Herodotus describes how it had come about, and then "Pausanias looked up to the precinct of Hera and called upon the goddess to let them not be cheated of their hope, and as he prayed, the omens turned favourable,"[31] and the men of Tegea and the Spartans charged home. That seizing of the moment puts him in the line of generals that has continued to Wellington and beyond. For the scene has its more secular counterpart when at Salamanca Wellington, after being outmarched and almost outmanoeuvred by Marmont, saw that at last his chance had come and said to his Spanish aide-de-camp, "Mon cher Alava, Marmont est perdu."

[30] E. Kirsten, "Athener und Spartaner in der Schlacht bei Plataiai," *Rhein. Mus.* LXXXVI, 1937, pp. 50 ff.
[31] Herod. IX, 61–62.

I have cited the instances of Miltiades and Pausanias because they show in these two Greeks what is of all the gifts of a general the one which owes most to nature and least to training. But the glory was not theirs alone. It is more significant still for the history of the Greek art of war that "the men who fought at Marathon" remained for generations the inspiration of the Athenians,[32] and that Aeschylus when he speaks of Plataea calls it the victory of the "Dorian Spear,"[33] that is, of the hoplites of Sparta and Tegea. The memory of those two deliverances fortified for two generations the belief that the secret of victory lay with the hoplite phalanx. But this was only a first stage in the development of the art of war. This was destined to advance when, in land operations, a wider experience of warfare and a greater variety of arms modified and enriched the traditional tactics of the city-state.

---

[32] Demosthenes, de Corona 208.

[33] Persae 817.

II

The Development of Infantry

As HAS been seen, the normal battle between hoplite armies ends, after a severe clash and some fighting at close quarters, in the rout of one side or the other. Pursuit is limited; the victor remains in possession of the battlefield, as though that was what he was fighting to possess. The vanquished accepts defeat: he is given his dead to bury: the victor sets up a trophy to mark his success. The recipe for victory is to have more *or* better, or more *and* better, hoplites than the opponent. Except for the successful exploitation of an advantage on the right wing—and this requires more tactical control than most generals could apply—the battle is a head-on collision all along the line. It would seem to follow that it is almost irrational to engage in battle unless the hoplite strength of the two sides approaches parity.

Is this the whole story? What other kinds of troops could a state provide that might make good an inferiority in hoplites, and how could they be used in battle or other operations of war? Suppose a state, though comparatively weak in hoplites, is strong in cavalry. In mediaeval warfare a relatively small force of armoured cavalry might defeat a large force of foot soldiers. But very few ancient Greek states were strong in cavalry, and none, in this period, could produce cavalry that could charge an unbroken phalanx of hoplites with any hope of success.[1]

Let us, for the time being, rule out cavalry and confine our

[1] The reasons for this will be found in the fourth lecture.

attention to infantry. What about missile weapons and those
who used them? Nowadays what really settles battles by land
or sea and wins a war is the missile in one form or another, the
bullet, the shell, the torpedo, the bomb in all its manifestations.
Was there nothing of that kind that could do the trick? What
about the javelin, the arrow, the slingstone or sling bullet, which
smite from afar? It is, of course, an attractive notion to smite
from afar, as did Paris when his arrow killed Achilles. In
Euripides' *Hercules Furens*[2] Amphitryon declares that the hoplite's life depends on the courage of his comrades, that if he
breaks his spear he has no defence, while an archer can loose up
to ten thousand arrows at his opponents. He stands far off and
wounds his enemies with unseen shafts and does not offer himself to be attacked but is secure. This is the most artful thing in
battle, to harm your enemy and preserve your own life. The
point is well taken; but what of the myriad arrows and standing
so far off? An archer could carry in his quiver fifteen to twenty
arrows (I would like to see a quiver that could carry a myriad),
and the range of the Greek bow was probably from eighty to a
hundred yards,[3] far less than the range of the English longbow
of the Middle Ages, which was drawn in a different way.
Arrows would not go through shields—at least it is a portent
to Xenophon when some mountaineers with much bigger bows
than the Greeks used could make their arrows pierce the shields
and corslets of the Ten Thousand.[4] So much for archers. The
range of a javelin was only some twenty yards: it had slight
penetrating power and a man could carry only a few of them.
There is a little more to be said for slingers. Good slingers could
slightly outrange archers, and they could carry a few fairly
heavy stones or up to fifty leaden sling bullets. But the sling is

---

[2] 188–203. Wilamowitz-Moellendorf (*Herakles*, I, p. 344) points out the relevance of
this passage to the military ideas of the time.

[3] The details of the range etc. of missile weapons are given by W. Rüstow–H. Köchly,
Geschichte des griechischen Kriegswesens von der ältesten Zeit bis auf Pyrrhos, p. 129.

[4] *Anab.* IV, 2. 28.

not a weapon of precision except in the hands of men who had used it from boyhood. And it was not easy to bring any very large number of slingers into play on a battlefield; for each slinger has to have a good deal of elbow room, or he impinges upon his neighbour's sphere of action or even his neighbour's head. To take Amphitryon's other point, that the archer is safe from harm in battle; his fire cannot hold up a charge of hoplites, for they are well protected and their charge is a matter of minutes. If the archer stands his ground, he is a dead man, and even if he runs away he may not escape. Archers and their like could be effective in mountainous country or in the defence and attack of a city wall, but in a pitched battle they soon shot their bolt and achieved little while doing so.

Thus in most Greek armies of the earlier classical period light-armed troops were not regarded as of serious military value. To be effective they needed much training—more perhaps than any hoplite,—great courage, and good leadership.[5] Without these they were hardly worth their rations as soldiers, though they might be used on the outskirts of war to carry the shields of their betters, or to devastate a hostile countryside. They had a future, as will be seen, but in the battles of the hoplite armies they hardly had a present. Thus, with cavalry comparatively rare and light-armed troops as lightweight as their weapons, the phalanx remained the queen of the battlefield. And so, in much of Greece, things might have gone on in the old way until the last hoplite had fought his last battle. But in fact the art of war did not stand still: there were changes in land warfare, and the causes and character of these is my next topic.

In the last third of the fifth century came the long-drawn struggle between Athens and most of the rest of Greece that is

---

[5] Thucydides (IV, 94, 1) is aware of the disadvantage of not having a properly trained corps of light-armed troops. See also Xen. *Mem*. III, 5, 2–5. At Athens the Thetes could be used as rowers in the fleet. But it is worth noting that the advent of democracy (e.g. at Argos) did not in itself weaken the belief in the primacy of hoplites.

compendiously called the Peloponnesian War. Before the first summer of that war was over, it had become plain that it would not be decided by a great pitched battle on land. For Athens did not need to fight such a battle in order to survive, and her enemies, though superior in strength, could not force her to fight it against her will. With the command of the sea and her impregnable linked fortress of Athens and the Piraeus she could not be starved into surrender. There was, in the eighth year of the war, a pitched battle between the Athenians and the Boeotians, but it was almost an accident[e] and is an exception that proves the rule. But in this first decade of the war there were a series of minor operations, not on the stage proper, but in the wings. And these showed the value of light-armed troops in a terrain that suited them. I will take the two most striking instances.

The Athenian general Demosthenes was persuaded to invade the mountainous country of Aetolia. He was told that though the Aetolian people were numerous and warlike they lived in scattered, unwalled villages, and were only light-armed troops, so that they could easily be subdued piecemeal. He advanced with allied infantry and three hundred Athenian hoplites, without waiting for some light-armed troops, which was what he was short of. For, says Thucydides, the fact that chance had been on his side hitherto made him optimistic. The Aetolians had gathered their forces and attacked his army with javelins, they retired when it advanced against them, and when it retired they returned to the attack. And so the battle went on, an alternation of pursuits and withdrawals, with the Athenians getting the worst of it in both. While the archers on the Athenian side still had arrows left and the opportunity to use them, they held out; for the Aetolians, having no defensive armour, did not stand up to their fire. But the commander of

---

[e] The battle of Delium; see below, pp. 84 f.

the archers was killed and the archers were scattered, and the Athenians were tired out with their constantly repeated efforts. The Aetolians then pressed upon them with their volleys of javelins. Then they turned and took flight. And they stumbled into ravines from which they could not climb up again and got lost in the unfamiliar ground, and many were destroyed by the javelins of the enemy that caught them up in flight. Most of them lost their way and got into the pathless woods, and the Aetolians brought fire and ringed them round with flames. Every kind of flight and every kind of destruction was their lot, and the survivors hardly won their way back to the sea whence they had started. There fell many allies and about a hundred and twenty Athenian hoplites—"the best soldiers of Athens that perished in this war."[7]

I have given this account from Thucydides because it shows the strength and weaknesses of the different kinds of troops in mountainous country. Demosthenes took the lesson to heart In the very next year he had to plan the attack on a smallish force of formidable Spartan hoplites marooned on the rocky island of Sphacteria.[8] By bringing against them contingents of light-armed troops from places where that kind of fighting had long been practised he wore down the resistance of the Spartans, who—to the amazement of Greece—surrendered. It was a most notable success, of military significance and of great diplomatic advantage to Athens. Earlier than this, light-armed troops acting with cavalry had routed a fine force of Athenian hoplites in the open country of Chalcidice.[9]

Before the whole war ended it was clear to those who had eyes to see—among them Thucydides[10]—that, though it was still true that hoplites mattered most in a set battle on a large scale,

---

[7] Thuc. III, 94–98.
[8] Thuc. IV, 29 ff.
[9] Thuc. II, 79.
[10] A. Bauer, "Ansichten des Thukydides über Kriegführung," *Philologus*, L (N.F. IV), 1891, pp. 401 ff.

war on land now had a place for other arms and other methods than those of the hoplite phalanx. Specialist light-armed troops rose in value. At sea also, as the war went on, skilled oarsmen were hired by both sides. And thus, the military potential of Greek states became more varied in character, and the way was open for new developments in the art of war. Cavalry remained an arm which only a few states could command, but by the fourth century the employment of professional troops on land affected both strategy and tactics and called for capacities in the handling of troops more specialized than had been hitherto apparent in Greek warfare.

It will be convenient if I discuss first the supply of such professional troops, and then their use, their tactics, and their command. Greek mercenaries were no new thing. For many years, besides the idea of the citizen fighting, on occasion, for his city, there had been the idea of soldiering as a profession, the practice of arms as a means of livelihood and an avenue of adventure.[11] It was, one may say, a form of craftsmanship to sell to those who would pay for it. As Greeks were ready to wander as traders, so they would go far afield to sell their swords or spears and the skill to use them. While citizen hoplites normally fought near home and only for short periods, the profession of a mercenary was not limited in time or space. Antimenides, the brother of the poet Alcaeus,[12] who, fighting for the Babylonians, overthrew a gigantic champion, the Greeks who scratched their names on the column at Abu Simbel far up the Nile[13]—these were soldiers of fortune, adventurers in arms. The famous song of Hybrias the Cretan[14] is the *credo* of such an adventurer.

[11] See, in general. H. W. Parke, *Greek Mercenary Soldiers from the Earliest Times to the Battle of Ipsus.* The process may have begun on a large scale with the Ionians, who supplied mercenaries to the Saïte kings in Egypt. See W. W. Tarn, *Hellenistic Military and Naval Developments*, p. 9.

[12] Alcaeus frag. 50 Diehl.

[13] Tod, *Greek Hist. Inscr.* 4.

[14] Diehl, *Anth. Lyr. Graec.* II, pp. 128–129.

In Greece itself, the overpopulated glens of Arcadia[15] found many sturdy men, some of good family, who left their homes to fight for employers in Greece or overseas, as the household troops of Persian satraps or of Greek tyrants. For such stalwarts the Greeks of the fifth century found the euphemism "auxiliaries" (*epikouroi*), mercenaries though they were.[16] During the Peloponnesian War many Greeks who had learned to fight had unlearned the arts of peace or found little scope for using them. Thus it was possible for the Younger Cyrus to hire ten thousand soldiers, most of them hoplites, to march with him to take from his brother King Artaxerxes the throne of Persia. He had to win one great battle, and for that he needed hoplites, while cavalry and light-armed troops could be found in the part of the Persian Empire he controlled. When he met his brother's army the Greek hoplites were irresistible but in the wrong place, and Cyrus lost his battle and his life.

Then the long march from before Babylon to the coast of the Black Sea taught the Ten Thousand to adapt themselves to many forms of war with the courageous resourcefulness of their nation and their leaders, above all, Xenophon. The military capacities of the Greek soldier could hardly have had a better advertisement. The Persians increasingly used Greek mercenaries, "the hair of the dog that bit them"; but there still remained in Greek lands many men who needed a livelihood and found one in soldiering.

With the variegation of warfare, such men might be trained to be light-armed troops and specialists in the use of this or that kind of missile weapon.[17] They had models in Greek communities such as the javelinmen of Aetolia who have been mentioned, but still more among barbarian peoples, who had

---

[15] Parke, *op. cit.* p. 11 n. 3 and p. 14.

[16] *Ibid.* p. 20

[17] The evidence on light-armed troops before the Hellenistic Age is well collected by O. Lippelt, *Die griechischen Leichtbewaffneten bis auf Alexander den Grossen*, Diss. Jena, 1910.

for generations used such weapons in their own wars and in the pay of other powers. In Thrace, above all, there had developed a resourceful technique of missile warfare. Thracians were indeed barbarians; they ate butter, which showed they were. They appear, to suit the comic purposes of Aristophanes, in the *Acharnians* as brutal and licentious soldiery;[18] and this they may have been. They might be without mercy, like those Thracian mercenaries who stirred the compassion of Thucydides when they massacred the women and children and even the very animals in the streets of the harmless little town of Mycalessus.[19] But war is a violent preceptor and taught civilized states to use such men. And with good leading and firm discipline they could be made trustworthy fighters, whatever else they were.

As the hoplites took their name from their shields, so these troops on the Thracian model were called peltasts from the name of their small, light target—which left them nimble to find safe room for the use of their throwing-spears. The islands also produced good slingers, especially Rhodians, and good archers, especially those of the island of Crete who could be hired to fight in any quarrel. The Persians were taught to draw the bow and speak the truth. It is the almost unanimous verdict of antiquity that it was idle to try to teach Cretans to speak the truth; but they had taught themselves to draw the bow with especial skill. It is in general true that mercenaries used in Greece tended more and more to be light-armed troops, especially peltasts. They were apt to fight in rather small formations under professional leaders. These could direct their more varied tactics and inspire in them an *esprit de corps* which could emulate the large-scale community self-confidence of the citizen phalanx. They could fight when the phalanx could not find level ground enough for its deployment, and now and then

[18] Vv. 156–166.
[19] VII, 29, 4.

they even won resounding successes against hoplites of high quality.

The chief hero of such exploits was the fourth-century Athenian general, Iphicrates, who raised and trained peltasts—now not only Thracians. Probably in the later stages of his career he improved their equipment and arms,[20] so that for anything but a great pitched battle they were the most effective infantry of the day. They may be compared with the riflemen whom Sir John Moore trained up to do what the redcoats of the line, for all their stubborn bravery, had not the mobility or the marksmanship to achieve in open warfare or in a war of ambushes where slow-moving troops might come to harm. Such troops as the Greek mercenaries became could be used to garrison strongholds or fortified positions,[21] for they could be continuously employed, as citizen troops could not be. And, having no homes, they were not always longing to return to them. And through the winter they could earn their retaining fee, while citizen troops were accustomed to fight only in the good season of the year.

Mercenaries had not the local patriotism of the citizen troops, but that made them, as it were, unpolitical. And so they could serve the purposes of Greek tyrants as they served the purposes of Persian kings and satraps. They were loyal to their paymasters and they had no republican principles which could make a tyrant distrust them. In the army of Dionysius I, tyrant of Syracuse, large forces of mercenaries were a counterpoise to the aristocratic cavalry for which that city was famous. And the same is true of the army of the Thessalian tyrant, Jason of Pherae. They could be taught to use the new engines of war that were coming into fashion. And, finally, while the lives of citizen soldiers were precious in the eyes of their cities, mercenaries were, to use a cold-blooded word, "expendable."

[20] Diod. XV, 44, 3; Cornelius Nepos, *Iphicrates* 1. See Parke, *op. cit.* pp. 76 ff.
[21] G. T. Griffith, *The Mercenaries of the Hellenistic World*, p. 71.

The adventuring abroad of Greeks as mercenaries before the close of the fifth century can hardly have meant a significant reduction of the military potential of Greece Proper in terms of troops. But it may have taken away some soldiers of native initiative who might have advanced the art of war if they had stayed at home. In the first half of the fourth century there may have been a rough balance between the mercenaries enlisted by Greek states from at home and abroad and those who left Greek lands to serve with foreign armies.

The mercenaries of Sicilian tyrants were in part drawn from the barbarians of the west who would otherwise have remained outside the range of Greek warfare. When a small force of such troops were sent by Dionysius I to help his Spartan allies, their virtuosity was a revelation to the Greeks of the homeland.[22] Still more important was the effect on warfare of the captains who led mercenary bands in the service of Greek states. They were not merely the tough fighting generals praised by Archilochus:[23] they were men of resource and sagacity, who knew how to manage their hard-bitten troops and outwit their opponents. The tricks of the trade which are preserved in collections of stratagems like those of Polyaenus[24] are often the inventions of these mercenary captains. And city-state generals who went off to fight with foreign armies, like Iphicrates and Chabrias of Athens, Pammenes of Thebes, the successor to Epaminondas, and even a veteran Spartan king, Agesilaus, must have learnt something in the course of their military travels. The experiments which Iphicrates made in the armament of peltasts appear to follow his return from campaigning in Egypt. The writings of Xenophon on the art of war, including the speculations which diversify his romance, the *Cyropaedeia,* are written by a soldier who had learnt his trade in the Retreat of the Ten

[22] Xen. *Hell.* VII, 1, 21.
[23] Frag. 60 Diehl³; see below, p. 83.
[24] See especially those attributed to Iphicrates.

Thousand. In the Hellenistic period the wars increasingly reveal the inventiveness of mercenary captains—above all, of that compound of artfulness, courage, and military experience, Bolis the Cretan, who is so well described in the eighth book of Polybius.[25] It is true that the use of mercenaries and their leaders tended to slow down the tempo of Greek warfare, for they were not inclined to seek decision by battle, for fear peace might break out. But they did, without doubt, advance the art of war and serve the original ideas of Greek and Macedonian generals, and help to variegate the composition and tactics of their armies.

The better trained and the better handled light troops became, the more they were an integral part of an army in the field. We find experiments in the use in battle of troops of all arms. This was more possible because light-armed mercenaries were more capable of manoeuvre than a phalanx of citizen hoplites, and their performance could be better calculated in advance. They might not meet the occasion with the high spirit of citizen soldiers, as Aristotle observes in his *Nicomachean Ethics*.[26] But once you had an army which combined professional skill with a national spirit and was led by a general of the first rank, the art of war in battle was bound to change. And before the middle of the fourth century this combination was provided in the form of the Macedonian army of Philip II.

But before that day came, there arose a soldier who was the greatest tactical innovator that the Greek city-states ever produced, Epaminondas. His native city, Thebes, had always been less conservative in the handling of its troops than other cities. The expertness of Sparta was content to play the old tunes with the old virtuosity. The Athenian Xenophon showed in his *Anabasis* how adaptable a Greek army could be made and in

[25] See 17, 1: "who was regarded as a man of exceptional intelligence, courage, and unsurpassed military experience."

[26] III, 1116 b 15. See Parke, *op. cit.* p. 137.

his writings pointed the way to improvements in the technique of warfare. But it was reserved for Thebes to produce in Pelopidas that rare phenomenon a good cavalry general, and in Epaminondas a man who could change the face of the hoplite battle by a tactical reform which ranks with, or above, the oblique order of Frederick the Great.

This was, like most great innovations in war, simple but demanding much skill in application. Epaminondas had to face a Spartan-led army. He could confidently expect that the right wing of the enemy would consist of the best Spartan troops. And *they* could confidently expect to gain the advantage on their right wing, and then, wheeling inwards, roll up the enemy line. As they had done so often before, they would win the battle before the less skilled allied contingents of their left and centre could lose it. Epaminondas ranged his Theban hoplites in a deep column. This was not without precedent, for the Thebans had done that, though to a lesser degree, in other battles. What was unprecedented was that he put his striking force on his left and held back the rest of his line. His column was irresistible and won the battle before *his* weaker troops of the centre and right could lose it.[27]

The traditional Spartan plan was refuted by this single stroke, so forceful and so surprising. If I may venture on a frivolous parallel—a farmer sought to administer a powder to his horse by blowing it into the horse's mouth, but the paradoxical animal blew first. If the essence of tactics is to place the maximum force at the crucial point, then, in this battle of Leuctra, Epaminondas exhibited tactics of a skill and force hitherto unknown in the history of war. In one short clash the century-old legend of Spartan invincibility was dispelled, as was the legend of Spanish invincibility at Rocroi, and the legend of Prussian invincibility at Valmy.

---

[27] See below, p. 76.

I now turn to Macedon. The second new stage in the history of infantry was the Macedonian phalanx. About the time that Philip II became king of Macedon, or just before, the Macedonian peasants were first organized as a fighting force. The army of Macedon was the king's army and its strength had lain in the cavalry that were called his *Companions,* as one may say, the Household Cavalry. Now there emerges as it were the Household Infantry, for they were given the name of the Foot Companions. They now received regular training, and were divided into battalions large enough to act independently at need but able to act together in the phalanx *par excellence* of the ancient world. They had longer spears than the Greek hoplites, and smaller shields,[28] and were not in deep formation, for they relied less on a charge and more on a steady advance, with a moving hedge of points to thrust back the enemy.[29] There was to be a day when the phalanx became, as it were, muscle-bound and without flexibility, and when its spears became too long for its mobility. Once in line of battle it could not form a flank or reverse the direction of its back ranks. If it could be upset it had the vulnerability of a hedgehog that is turned over. In fact it needed protection on its flanks from other troops. But, in its earlier days, it could advance with a more open or in a closer order, and its articulation in battalions "gave it legs," as was said at the time. In its advance it could bear down an enemy, but it was essentially a formation to be used with other arms. And in fact its most characteristic use was to pin down a part of the enemy line while the cavalry attacked in the flank or rear. It was a holding force rather than a striking force. In the army of Alexander the Great it was linked to the cavalry by a body of picked troops called hypaspists, who remained an eminent *corps d'élite.*

---

[28] See W. W. Tarn, *Hellenistic Military and Naval Developments,* p. 12.

[29] A difficulty which beset the phalanx was to preserve the alignment of its battalions so as not to offer a gap to an enemy. See the criticisms of Polybius XVIII, 28–33, especially 31–33. See Tarn, *op. cit.* pp. 13 f.

The tactical effect of the phalanx in its earliest phase may be illustrated from the first battle in which we can see it in action, the battle of Chaeronea.[80] The Greek army, mainly of Athenian and Theban hoplites, had staked all on a battle in a well-chosen defensive position. They must not expose their flanks to the strong cavalry of the enemy; so their left, the Athenians, were protected by high ground and the town of Chaeronea, and their right, the Thebans, by a river. So long as they preserved their alignment they might hope to repel the attack of the Macedonian infantry and win the battle. Philip had to create a weak point in their line. He commanded the phalanx on his right himself; his left, which presumably included the cavalry held in reserve, was put under the young prince Alexander. When the battle was joined, Philip caused his well-trained phalanx to carry out that most difficult manoeuvre—a deliberate fighting withdrawal. The Athenians were drawn on into a triumphal advance until the slope of the ground was in the Macedonians' favour. Their allies clung to the protection they had for their right flank, and so a gap was opened in their line and into this Alexander charged. At the same moment Philip caused the phalanx to stop withdrawing and attack, and the battle was over. He had by this skilful use of the phalanx created, as it were, a flank where no flank had been. And he had achieved also what Napoleon[81] said was one of the most difficult manoeuvres in battle, the going over from defence to attack with great speed and force at the right moment. This, then, is an illustration of what could be done by the phalanx in the hands of a master.

The two innovations which have been described meant, in the tactics of Epaminondas, the giving of new life and vigour

---

[80] See J. Kromayer, *Antike Schlachtfelder*, I, pp. 127 ff.; H. Delbrück, *Geschichte der Kriegskunst*, I³, pp. 175 f.; N. G. L. Hammond, "The Two Battles of Chaeronea (338 B.C. and 86 B.C.)," *Klio*, XXXI, 1938, pp. 186 ff.

[81] L. E. Henry, *Napoleon's War Maxims*, p. 23.

to the operations of a hoplite army; and meant, in the creation of the Macedonian phalanx, the promise of a new kind of battle technique in which the phalanx did not play the decisive part but which required the phalanx to make possible the decisive entry of cavalry as the striking force. The transition from the older battle to the new lies above all in the possibility of winning not by evenly applied pressure along all the line but by dedicating to the actual achievement of victory one special part of the army engaged. Here for a time we can leave infantry and turn to other forms of military force. But before we do so it is time to consider the other element in war, to leave the land and go faring on the sea and examine the problems of naval warfare.

III
Naval Warfare

IN MY first two lectures I did not discuss the manufacture of weapons, for the ancient art of war did not greatly depend on the character of weapons, apart from certain dimensions of shield and spear. Of Virgil's recipe for war "arms and the man," the second ingredient is what mattered. But naval warfare does depend very much indeed on the kind of ships you have. The last half century has shown the dreadnought, the fast destroyer, the submarine, the aircraft carrier each changing the face of naval warfare. There was no such rapid development in ancient ships, and could not be, with their limited material resources. But there were improvements in ships and the way of handling them which are interesting and instructive if not of world-shaking importance. And so I will start with these.

Naval warfare, in a strict sense, begins when ships not only carry men on warlike expeditions, but also are themselves instruments of war. This they may be either as a means to enable the fighting men on board to attack the crews and fighting men of other ships with missiles or boarding parties, or as a means of injuring other ships by being driven against their hulls or oarage. In the Heroic Age ships appear as transports, the servants of land warfare. They carry the Achaeans to the coasts of Troy, and they lie on the shore awaiting the day of return, or carry raiding parties to collect plunder or supplies. There is no hint in the *Iliad* that the Trojans had ships which might have forced the Achaeans to fight at sea.[1] The Heroic Age ships may use oars as well as sails, and in the post-Heroic Age ships become capable of fighting against each other. When that happens, the art of naval warfare begins.

It is roughly true to say that ships are now built to sail with the occasional use of oars, or to be rowed with the occasional use of sails. The second type prevails as ships of war, and by the seventh century there are ships which can manoeuvre against each other. For boarding or the use of missiles they have a kind of deck which can carry fighting men. But, besides that, the construction of these oar-driven ships leads to a strengthening of their bows by bulkheads on either side of the forward end of the keel. These coalesce, as it were, into a ram which can be propelled against the hull or oarage of an enemy ship. What was, to begin with, a means of overcoming the resistance of the waves as ships were rowed at sea, or of protecting them against rocks as they came to land, becomes the means of direct conflict between ships, and the ram may be further armed with a kind of spear.

In the seventh and sixth centuries, to judge from the archaeological evidence,[2] ships used in warfare were more and more adapted to the use of the ram at the expense of the deck which carried fighting men. Thus fighting by boarding or missile weapons was sacrificed to greater speed and capacity for manoeuvre. This was achieved by increasing the number of oarsmen, by increasing the length of the ship and reducing its height above the water, and abandoning whatever deck or superstructure there had been. Thus the penteconter, driven by twenty-five oarsmen on each side of the ship, became the standard ship of war and the standard method of combat was the use of the ram. I may add that throughout this period there

---

[1] R. Carpenter, "The Greek Penetration of the Black Sea," *Amer. Journ. Arch.* LII, 1948, p. 6 n 1.

[2] G. S. Kirk, "Ships on Geometric Vases," *Ann. Brit. School at Athens*, XLIV, 1949, pp. 93 ff.

seems to have been a transient use of ships with two banks of
oars, probably borrowed from the Phoenicians, but this device
for increasing oarage, and so increasing speed, may have been
found unsuitable for the open sea and so was abandoned.

A critical examination of the slight literary evidence does not
refute, but in some measure confirms, the deductions that follow
from the archaeological evidence.[3] Then came a notable invention. The penteconters had served the ends of trade for distant
voyages as well as those of war. Now some unknown ship-
wright in the second half of the sixth century[4] devised a vessel
that was a warship and nothing else, and a warship of far
greater power than the Greeks had known before. It was the
trireme, which for nearly two centuries ruled the waves in
Greek naval warfare, and continued to be used for centuries
later.

It is certain that the trireme was rowed by many oarsmen—
as many as a hundred and seventy—each rowing one oar,[5] and
yet was not much longer than the penteconter with its fifty
rowers. It could not be much longer, for that would put too
great a strain upon the keel. How this result was attained is
still disputed. Fortunately for the present purpose, it is enough
to know that it was achieved. But it would be unduly timid of
me if I did not add that I belong to that hardy band who do not
believe that a trireme was rowed with three superimposed
banks of oars, but by a single tier of oars arranged in groups of
three as in the Venetian galleys of the Middle Ages.[6] On any
assumption, the crucial invention was probably that of the out-

---

[3] *Ibid.* p. 143.

[4] J. A. Davison, "The First Greek Triremes," *Class. Quart.* XLI, 1947, pp. 18 ff.

[5] Thuc. II, 93, 2.

[6] For the evidence for the view adopted in the text see W. W. Tarn, "The Greek
Warship," *Journ. Hell. Stud.* XXV, 1905, pp. 137 ff., 204 ff., and "The Oarage of
Greek Warships," *Mariner's Mirror*, XIX, 1933, pp. 52 ff.; F. Brewster, "The Arrange-
ment of Oars in the Trireme," *Harv. Class. Stud.* XLIV, 1933, pp. 205 ff. For a state-
ment of the rival view see J. S. Morrison, "The Greek Trireme," *Mariner's Mirror*,
XXVII, 1941, pp. 14 ff.

rigger to support the oars and even out their leverage. Anyhow, however it was done, a ship was produced that was swift and capable of manoeuvre, a ship that gave great scope for skilful rowing and steering, the ship itself being a kind of composite weapon, with mind directing matter to the confusion of the enemy.

Fleets appear in which ship fights ship. Soon after the middle of the sixth century we find this happening at the battle of Alalia, for the Phocaean penteconters which fought in that battle got their rams bent or were disabled in the fighting.[7] But the first battle in which large forces of triremes can be discovered seeking to exploit their capabilities is the battle of Lade in 494, which really decided the fate of the Ionian Revolt.[8] For a time before the battle the Ionians had practised manoeuvres that imply nimbleness and a general homogeneity in the ships. The Persian fleet prevailed because of desertions on the Greek side, so that the battle of Lade was no test of what Greek triremes could do.

Fourteen years later came the Great Persian War and, in the meantime, Athens had built a large fleet of warships of the new model. But it cannot be assumed that their rowers and steersmen had yet reached the full mastery of their instrument. Some at least of the Persian ships were probably more skilled in manoeuvre, and the Persian fleet had an advantage in numbers. In the first meeting of the two fleets, that in the Gulf of Artemisium, the Persians seems to have had rather the best of it, and it may be doubted if the Greeks used their ships to the fullest advantage. For victory they had to wait for the crowning mercy of Salamis, won by surprise, a determined onset, and the confusion of their enemy. How fortunate was the Athenian actor who, eight years later, declaimed the magnificent lines of Aeschylus to a theatre with thousands of hearers who heard

[7] Herod. I, 166.
[8] Herod. VI, 8–15.

described what they had done. The Persians had been led to
hope that the Greeks were bent upon escape.

> But, not as for flight
> Did the Greeks then raise their proud paean,
> But for the onset, full of heart and courage.[9]

Then of the Persians—

> The crowd of ships within the narrow strait
> Helpless to help each other, ship on ship,
> A mass of breaking oars and huddled craft,
> Themselves their ruin, their own brazen prows
> Grind them to death . . .[10]

It was not the Athenians alone who won the battle—their kins-
men had charged as bravely,—but the new Athenian navy had
justified the foresight of Themistocles, made good his strategy,
and turned back the tide of war.

In the year after Salamis the naval war was carried across
the Aegean. From now on for thirty years the Athenian fleet
and the squadrons of her allies needed to be used in amphibious
operations and would have to meet ships which probably had a
higher freeboard. Their admiral Cimon made a change in the
trireme by making it broader in the beam and giving it a kind
of bridge along its length so that it could carry more fighting
men.[11] With these ships he was very successful, but by the
middle of the century, when a *modus vivendi* was reached with
Persia, the Athenians were reverting to the older tactics of
ramming and had improved upon them. The fleets of the Confederacy of Delos had become more predominantly Athenian,
and those ships which were provided by the Allies would be
brought into line with Athenian construction and practice. Not
only had the Athenians the best ships, but the best oarsmen and,

---

[9] *Persae* 392–394.
[10] *Persae* 413–416.
[11] Plutarch, *Cimon* XII, 2. The precise character of the change is not above all doubt.

even more important, the best steersmen. Before the Peloponnesian War began there was a marked difference between the tactics and skill of the Athenian navy and those of other Greek states, so that in the battle of Sybota, where Corcyraean and Peloponnesian ships were engaged, the Athenians noted that they fought more as in a land battle with boarding and the use of missile weapons.[12]

Such methods as these had, by then, become out of place in the best naval circles. With the development of ship fighting against ship had come in the discovery of tactics which might exploit superior speed or capacity for manoeuvre. For example, the Greek word for circumnavigation was given the technical meaning of sailing round a ship or a line of ships so as to be able to attack the stern or a weak point in the side of enemy vessels. And there was something more direct, more Nelsonian as it were. This was the breaking through an enemy line by rowing between two opposing ships and then wheeling round to take one or other of them at a disadvantage before it could manoeuvre to meet this attack. This manoeuvre plainly called for high speed and, even more important, brilliant steering promptly supported by skilful oarsmanship. It was therefore, above all, the tactical device of highly trained crews in ships of the most skilful construction. A variant of this manoeuvre was to make the attacking trireme swerve so that its projecting bulkheads might sweep away the oars on one side of an opposing ship, while, just before the impact, the oarage of the near side of the attacking ship was drawn inwards out of harm's way. If this device succeeded, the victim was so crippled that it was out of the fight at the best, and destined to be sunk later at the worst. Of all these tactical manoeuvres the Athenians became masters in the heyday of their naval skill.

It was taken as axiomatic that Athenian naval power could

---

[12] Thuc. I, 49, 1–3.

only be rivalled by the acquiring of Athenian technique, and this was beyond the capacity, if not beyond the hopes, of her most sanguine opponents. When a superior Peloponnesian fleet met the squadron of the Athenian admiral Phormio, they had to put their trust in courage, while the Athenian crews trusted in the silent and swift carrying out of skilful manoeuvres, which, by their very boldness, proved their admitted superiority.[18] The course of the first engagement illustrates this. Phormio with twenty triremes finds in the early morning forty-seven Peloponnesian ships, some carrying troops, seeking to cross from the Peloponnese to the opposite shore. These form a circle with prows pointing outwards, so that any Athenian trireme that tries to strike at one of their ships will not have the sea room to manoeuvre and can be attacked by five picked ships that are within the circle. So long as the ships preserve their formation they are comparatively secure, though indeed it is not easy to see how they will make headway towards their destination. Phormio is aware that a breeze will soon blow in from the open sea. He first forms his fleet in line ahead and rows round the enemy circle, feinting to attack. And at each feint the circle tends to narrow as the Peloponnesian ships draw back from the expected blow. Then comes the breeze, and the circle is in confusion, and the Athenian triremes take their chances and make havoc among the enemy who are almost defenceless as they try to keep away from each other. They break and take to flight as best they can and the Athenians capture twelve of them, crews and all.

The engagement that followed not long after shows another picture. The defeated Peloponnesian fleet was reinforced not only with ships but with the advice of Brasidas, the most resourceful officer Sparta ever produced. Phormio had asked for reinforcements, but they had not arrived. Now the enemy fleet

---

[18] Thuc. II, 83 ff.

four abreast rowed parallel with his twenty ships, as they moved in single line ahead. And then at a given signal the Peloponnesians wheeled and charged, and so drove part of the Athenian fleet back against the coast behind them. The leading eleven ships evaded the attack by hard rowing and twenty Peloponnesian ships joyfully pursued them. The day seemed lost, and then the last of the Athenian ships rowed round a merchant ship lying at anchor and rammed the side of the leading pursuer and sank it. And as its companions halted in confusion, then, says Thucydides, "daring seized the Athenians and at a single word of command they charged," and so they retrieved the battle. The brilliant use of the circumnavigation of the merchantman was perhaps the highlight of Athenian seamanship, and one would like to conjecture that Phormio himself was in that trireme.

The first ten years of the war indeed mark the zenith of Athenian skill at sea, even if the fleet that set out on the Sicilian Expedition, six years later, was the finest that ever sailed from the Piraeus. It was never to return. In the relatively confined space of the Great Harbour at Syracuse the swifter, more lightly built Athenian triremes were at a disadvantage against enemy ships more suited to survive when ship met ship prow to prow. We may conjecture that the peace which preceded the Expedition permitted the Corinthians to hire more skilled oarsmen, and at last a Corinthian squadron in Greek waters was able to meet an Athenian force on equal terms.[14] The disaster at Syracuse swept away so many fine ships and crews that the unchallengeable supremacy of Athens at sea disappeared. The defection of allies reduced the area of recruitment of rowers for Athens and increased it for her enemies. A Syracusan squadron brought the inspiration of a victory, and Persian subsidies presently helped to pay for Peloponnesian fleets. Even so, the seamanlike skill of Athenian captains in using the current

---

[14] Thuc. VII, 34.

through the Dardanelles won the battle of Cynossema,[15] a skilful surprise won the battle of Cyzicus,[16] and a formation designed to make good the decline in tactical nimbleness won the battle of Arginusae. An eminent writer on naval tactics, Admiral Custance, points out that this engagement was won, not by skilful manoeuvres of each ship, but by skill in throwing masses of ships into battle, and by hard fighting, so that Arginusae was the prototype of Trafalgar.[17] And then the sanguine spirit that refused to make the best obtainable peace after two victories, and the indiscipline and carelessness that left the last Athenian fleet open to a surprise at Aegospotami, made Athens helpless at sea and therefore helpless altogether.

The period of Athenian naval ascendancy was the most striking of the periods for which the Greeks found the word *thalassocracy*—the command of the sea. Pericles, always perhaps more an admiral than a general, realized, like the unknown author of the contemporary pamphlet on the *Constitution of Athens*,[18] and perhaps overestimated, the scope and effectiveness of sea power, especially in time of war. It could secure the safe transit of food from the south of Russia to the wharves of the Piraeus. It could greatly hinder enemy trade passing up the Saronic Gulf, or along the Gulf of Corinth so long as there was a naval station near its entrance. It could convoy Athenian armies to any part of the Athenian Empire and carry raiding forces to any point on and off the coast of the Peloponnesus.

So far thalassocracy in war. But triremes and fleets of triremes had limitations which it is easy to forget.[19] They could not carry

---

[15] Thuc. VIII, 104–106; Diod. XIII, 39–40; see W. L. Rodgers, *Greek and Roman Naval Warfare*, p. 179, R. Custance, *War at Sea*, pp. 40 ff.

[16] Xen. *Hell.* I, 1, 13–19; Diod. XIII, 50; Plutarch, *Alcibiades* 28.

[17] Custance, *op. cit.* p. 109.

[18] II, 6 ff.

[19] See *C.A.H.* V, p. 195; A. W. Gomme, *Essays in Greek History and Literature*, pp. 190 ff., and *Historical Commentary on Thucydides, Book I*, pp. 19 f.

food and water for long voyages or afford reasonable comfort for the crowded crews. They were blind at night and had poor means of communication at sea. They lay low in the water,[20] and even if they were proceeding under sail they had not tall masts to help them watch out for the enemy or signal to each other. When they were operating as fighting fleets and nothing else, they carried too few marines to secure a landing on a hostile coast without serious risk. They might, in favourable conditions, blockade a harbour, but they could not blockade a long coastline. Their power of preventing the movement of enemy armies by sea was precarious. I can think of only two instances in Greek history of the destruction of enemy transports by a superior fleet.[21] Warships were expensive to maintain, for their crews were large, and their losses in men in any hard-fought battle[22] were not easily replaced, even granted that superior skill might enable comparatively small fleets to be sure of victory. The ships themselves rapidly deteriorated unless they were well housed whenever they were not on active service, and they had much to fear from bad weather when they were. For they were frail: they have been well compared to glorified racing eights.[23] However suited triremes were to manoeuvre against their own kind, they were less effective against sturdy sailing merchant ships, for if a trireme rammed a merchant ship it might not survive its success: a merchantman with a following wind could give a trireme a long chase, and merchantmen could take to the open sea for great distances while triremes must keep fairly near to land. All this must be remembered,

---

[20] E.g. a man wading could climb into a trireme that was just afloat. Thuc. II, 90, 6.

[21] Leptines against Carthaginians (Diod. XIV, 55); Cleitus against Nicanor (*ibid.* XVIII, 72; Polyaenus IV, 6, 8).

[22] For a list of losses in sea battles see H. Droysen, *Heerwesen und Kriegführung der Griechen*, p. 308 n. 2.

[23] W. W. Tarn, *Hellenistic Military and Naval Developments*, p. 124. He adds: "That is an exaggeration, of course, but it is one which I have found useful myself as a better line of approach to the matter than the modern associations of the word 'ship.'"

and it may be a matter of some surprise that triremes ruled the waves for as long as they did.

In the fourth century fleets were smaller, but, even so, it was a great strain on Athens to recover from her relative weakness at sea in the middle third of the century. And though triremes never quite lost their usefulness, they gradually ceased to be the standard ship of the line. Early in the fourth century Dionysius I of Syracuse is credited with the construction of some larger ships,[24] though their number and their effectiveness were probably exaggerated by the ancient authorities. But by the time of Alexander the Great there was coming into service the successor to the trireme, the quinquereme, and, quite soon, ships of even greater power. These ships are defined by numerical designations which indicate the ratio of their oar power, however it was applied. They may be called, for instance, fivers, sixers, seveners and so on. Quinqueremes were now rowed by long oars or sweeps in one single row with five men pulling each oar; ships of higher denominations are rowed with more men to an oar or also more oars, however they are grouped.

The problem how ships of definitely higher denominations could have been rowed has not been solved beyond doubt,[25] and this is not the occasion to try to solve it in detail. If we suppose, as is reasonable, that the trireme had had the maximum oar power that its construction would stand, the new increase of oar power should mean some further strengthening of the hull. What is common to the larger ships is that they are called *cataphracts,* which means that the rowers were covered in and protected by an overhead deck. This deck may have added to the strength of the ship's structure so that it could resist the strain of so much more oarage power. Besides that, it made it possible to have a platform for large boarding parties of troops

---

[24] Tarn, *op. cit.* pp. 130 ff.; A. Bauer, *Griech. Kriegsaltertümer*[2], pp. 417 f.

[25] Tarn, *op. cit.* pp. 134 ff.

who might be one hundred strong or more, compared with the fourteen marines on an Athenian trireme in the Peloponnesian War. The rowing would require many oarsmen but most of them less skilled than in the heyday of trireme tactics. Manoeuvre would be slower and less resourceful. On the other hand, from Alexander onward it was easier to find well-trained infantry than skilled oarsmen. When Rome became a first-class naval power this suited her military potential, and the danger to her fleets in her early seagoing enterprises was due rather to a lack of seamanlike competence and caution than to the action of the enemy. Prince Rupert was accused, not wholly with justice, of handling a fleet as though it was a troop of horse: it would be a juster reproach that Roman consuls were apt to handle a fleet as though it was a legion. And it is interesting to observe that in his great naval victory of Salamis in Cyprus, Demetrius adopted the land tactics of the day, and struck home with his left wing and then rolled up the enemy line exactly as generals were seeking to do with their striking force of cavalry.[26] All this did not mean that lighter and swifter vessels lost their value for war and for the policing of the seas, and, on occasion, there appeared fleets of triremes and of lesser craft which operated with the great ships or in place of them. Naval tactics and naval construction thus went hand in hand, and both Pompey and Agrippa—and before them the Rhodians—realized the value of both kinds of vessels and made use of both.

I may now turn to the application of naval warfare in the field of strategy rather than of battle tactics. It is worth observing that if the comparative invisibility of ancient ships limited the value of command of the seas, this very invisibility could be used to gain a strategical advantage or to achieve surprise. Surprise is highly valued by all good judges of war, and the power to achieve it is one criterion of military or naval resourceful-

---

[26] Diod. XX, 50–52; Plutarch, *Demetrius* 16.

ness. Yet surprises are not common in Greek or Macedonian war by land or sea. It is on the whole true that the art of reconnaissance and the gathering of intelligence was not a strong point of fleets or armies in antiquity. To achieve surprise usually needs good intelligence, just as does the capacity to guard against it. Even so, it is to me surprising that armies and fleets were not oftener the victims of a well-planned surprise. I can only conjecture that ancient commanders, Roman as well as Greek and Macedonian, were reluctant to initiate the bold movement and take the calculated risk that often leads to catching the enemy unawares. From Thucydides[27] onwards the truth was proclaimed that in war there is, and must be, a large element of the unexpected. It may be that ancient generals and admirals feared this as an enemy rather than sought to use it as a friend and ally.

But there is a strategy which depends on the use of fleets and their power of moving troops quickly and quietly. Thus in the early years of the fifth century the Spartan king Cleomenes manoeuvred his Argive opponents out of a strong position by transshipping his troops under cover of darkness to the opposite coast so that he could advance on Argos from another side and force the enemy to meet him there.[28] Further, the dependence of fleets on land led to combined operations by armies and fleets, which afforded scope to the strategist. Thus in the Great Persian War the stand of Leonidas at Thermopylae had for its prime object the bringing about a naval battle in limited sea room so as to give the Greek fleet the hope of a victory which might halt the Persians' advance by land. The hope was not fulfilled, and Leonidas and his Spartans died in vain.

More fruitful was the shrewd strategy which posted the Greek fleet at Salamis on the flank of a Persian advance whether

[27] E.g. III, 30, 4.
[28] Herod. VI, 76–77.

by land or sea.[29] A Greek fleet at Salamis presented to the Persians the problem which an English fleet near Plymouth presented to the Spanish Armada as it sought to move up the Channel to reach the Prince of Parma in the Low Countries. The Persians tried to solve the problem by an attack which proved their ruin; the Spaniards disregarded it with no greater success.

In a yet wider field of naval strategy the island of Cyprus was an island of strategical importance with a mixed population of Greek and Oriental origin. That importance lay mainly in its geographical position. It was too far from the Greek waters of the Aegean to come within the scope of Hellenic politics or economics; but it lay near enough to the coast of Phoenicia to hamper the development of Persian naval strength, which was mainly based upon the sea power of that coast. Thus, if Cyprus was firmly controlled by Greek naval power, it went far to protect the eastern Aegean from the intrusion of Persian fleets. Twice—at the beginning of the fifth century and at the beginning of the fourth—the failure to make good the control of Cyprus as an advanced naval base was fatal to Greek hopes. In the Ionian Revolt the Greeks after a promising start let it escape their grasp,[30] and the Revolt failed because the Phoenician fleet was able to invade the Aegean in great strength. And, a century later, a similar failure induced by the skilful strategy of the Persian satraps in western Asia Minor, ended in a Persian naval victory that refuted the last Spartan hopes of maintaining themselves in Asia Minor and restored communications between the Persians and Greece.[31] Twice in the intervening century that sound strategist, the Athenian admiral Cimon, opened a naval attack on Cyprus.[32] The first time, after he had lost control of

[29] Custance, *op. cit.* p. 27.
[30] *C.A.H.* IV, p. 223.
[31] *C.A.H.* VI, p. 40.
[32] *C.A.H.* V, pp. 77, 87.

Athenian strategy, his ships were diverted to help an Egyptian revolt against Persia. The second time, he died before the venture reached complete success. But it did much to bring about a *modus vivendi* between Athens and Persia which precluded the advance of the Phoenician fleet into Greek waters and, for a generation, made the Aegean an Athenian lake. Nor does the story of Cyprus end there. The Persians were careful to recover complete control of it in what is called the King's Peace, though in their many preoccupations at the middle of the century it became independent, so that it could be of strategic value to Alexander and later to Antigonus I.[33] It was in the waters of Cyprus that his son, Demetrius, won a great naval victory,[34] and by then it had become the objective of the naval policy of the Ptolemies, for it served the ends of their sea power and was the halfway house between Egypt and her possessions in the Levant. In fact it does not cease to be disputed between naval powers until the general decline of the Hellenistic navies had set in late in the third century.

An even more important objective of Athenian naval policy was to secure for her commerce the passage of the Bosporus and the Dardanelles. Throughout the fifth and fourth centuries the corn that came to Athens from the northern shores of the Black Sea in return for Attic wares was a vital part of her food supply. Athens could not afford to see a hostile power in control of the Straits. These waters and the two islands of Lemnos and Imbros, the outer guard of the Dardanelles, were the constant preoccupation of Athenian diplomacy in peace and of Athenian strategy in war. During much of the fifth century this side of Athenian naval policy was merged in the general control of her Empire by sea. But it becomes clearer again in the last decade of the Peloponnesian War. For when her enemies got a footing on the west coast of Asia Minor the naval war tended to gravitate

---

[33] *C.A.H.* VI, pp. 54, 146 f., 249 f., 375, 486, 498.

[34] See above, p. 40.

towards the Dardanelles.[85] Her opponents had not failed to observe their importance, and the able Spartan admiral Mindarus transferred the naval war to that area by a daring move. It ended in disaster, but the final irreparable defeat of the Athenian navy in those parts made certain the surrender of Athens.

In the fourth century it was pressure on the Dardanelles that compelled the Athenians to acquiesce in the King's Peace, provided that their hold on Lemnos and Imbros was guaranteed.[86] The costly revival of Athenian naval strength later in the century was promoted by that cautious realist, Eubulus, because naval power was the one way of securing the very existence of Athens. Soon after this we can see the importance of the Straits as it appeared to another power than Athens. Philip II of Macedon wished to secure Athenian acquiescence at least in his Greek policy and moved against the strong cities of Perinthus and Byzantium, which commanded the passage of the Bosporus. If these were in his hands, the food supply of Athens would be highly precarious despite the superior strength of the Athenian navy. The Athenians were active to hinder his operations before Byzantium. At the same time, another factor in the problem of the Straits was underlined by the help which Persia hastened to give to Perinthus—for this act of Persia's must have been to forestall the somewhat remoter danger of a Macedonian invasion of Asia Minor. Despite his skill in siegecraft Philip failed to take either city, though a surprise assault on Byzantium was only foiled by the barking of incorruptible watchdogs. Thus the active defence of the Bosporus caused Philip to resort to direct operations against Athens. His victory at Chaeronea gave to him the control of Athenian policy and so the control of the Straits

---

[85] *C.A.H.* V, pp. 341 ff.

[86] F. Miltner, "Die Meerengenfrage in der griechischlkn Geschichte," *Klio*, XXVIII, 1935, pp. 1 ff.; F. Graefe, "Die Operationen des Antalkidas im Hellespont," *ibid*. pp. 262 ff.; W. Judeich in Pauly-Wissowa, *Realenc.* s.v. Antalkidas, col. 2344.

and opened the way to an invasion of Asia Minor. Each of these operations, that against Athens via the Straits and against the Straits via Athens, was a classical example of what has been called the strategy of indirect approach.[87]

Finally, the maintenance of naval power required access to the material for ships—above all, the heavy timber that was rare in the Mediterranean world,—and hides and pitch that were needed in shipyards. And these could be secured by naval power. As the author of the *Constitution of Athens* says: "If a city is rich in wood for shipbuilding, where will it be able to dispose of it without the permission of the ruler of the sea? And the same is true of iron or bronze or sailcloth, which very things are what ships are made of. And those who rule the sea can say where they are to go."[88] The naval requirements of Athens are reflected in her negotiations with Macedon in the fifth century in her desire to secure a prior claim on the relevant exports of that country.[89] So too in Hellenistic times the ambition of Egypt to be a great naval power was one cause of her desire to control Syria, where she could find the heavy timber which Egypt does not produce. This affected her foreign policy, just as in the Napoleonic Wars English strategy and foreign policy were affected by a strong desire to import from the forests of Scandinavia tall trees for the masts of Nelson's seventy-fours and tar to caulk their seams.

Finally, I should add a word about the interaction of sea and land in a wider setting. Since the work of Mahan on the influence of sea power on history, we have all been very conscious of the effect of naval strength on war by land. The Grand Army of Napoleon on the cliffs of Boulogne foiled by "the weather-beaten sails of distant ships on which their eyes never looked" is,

[87] B. H. Liddell Hart in the book of that name, London, 1941.

[88] II, 11; for the converse when Athens lost the command of the sea in 413 B.C. see Thuc. VIII, 1, 3.

[89] Tod, *Greek Hist. Inscr.* 66, ll. 35–41, see also Thuc. IV, 108, 1; for the fourth century see Xen. *Hell.* VI, 1, 4.

to me at least, a grateful and comforting thought. But, for reasons I have already given, ancient fleets could not exert this distant pressure. The fleets of Greece and Macedon, as indeed those of Rome, could better secure the movement of their own armies than hinder the movement of the armies of others. Still, the pressure of sea power might isolate or immobilize an army, even in antiquity. When the Athenians before Syracuse lost the battle in the Great Harbour, their army was lost with it. When the Greeks won the battle of Salamis, it meant the enforced reduction of the Persian army to a strength which was no longer invincible. The defeat of the Egyptian navy in the third century deprived the Ptolemies of their power of effective intervention in Greece Proper and the Aegean world.[40] But the military interaction of land and sea might work both ways, and the sea might be, as it were, conquered from the land.

I will take an example from the career of Alexander the Great. It was all-important for him to eliminate the powerful Persian navy which might otherwise make contact with Greece to his great danger. Alexander's way of achieving this was to get control of the west coast of Asia Minor and then that of Phoenicia, so that the crews of the Persian ships knew that they must choose between the service of the King of Persia and their return to their homes.[41] With its roots severed, the Persian fleet withered away. And the converse appears in Alexander's invasion of the Indus Valley. This was a land operation of the greatest possible range. But Alexander was careful to link with it a naval expedition under an able and resourceful admiral.[42] Not the least important element in the art of war is to be aware that naval power and land power may be friends and may be enemies, colleagues or rivals, as time and place may dictate, and to make the best use of both.

---

[40] See A. Koester in J. Kromayer–G. Veith, *Heerwesen und Kriegführung der Griechen und Römer*, pp. 173 ff.

[41] *C.A.H.* VI, p. 363.

[42] *Ibid.* pp. 403, 414 ff.

IV

Cavalry, Elephants, and Siegecraft

THE USE of horses to draw chariots goes out of Greek warfare before the classical period. War chariots continued to be used at Cyrene and Barce in North Africa, and at Eretria in Euboea sixty chariots continued to figure in some kind of parade or procession—but they hardly come into our story; they belong rather to the military history of the older Oriental monarchies. The one serious attempt to win a battle with chariots, with which we are concerned, was that of Darius at Gaugamela, and it was a complete failure. This was probably because Alexander's light-armed troops attacked them before they had worked up their full speed.[1] The same thing happened to the scythed chariots of Antiochus the Great at Magnesia, when he was fighting against the Romans. So I think we can bow them out, scythes and all. On the other hand, by the seventh century cavalry formed a regular part of the armed strength of a few states, especially where the country is open, as in Thessaly and, to a limited degree, in Boeotia and its neighbours. Cavalry can be traced later in Chalcidice and in Sicily, especially at Syracuse. Athens had an aristocratic force of knights, who ride so proudly on the frieze of the Parthenon, and, for a time, some mounted archers. In Macedon the gentry and their personal followers formed the forerunners of the famous Companion

[1] W. W. Tarn, *Hellenistic Military and Naval Developments*, p. 20.

cavalry of Alexander the Great. In Asia Minor some cities had horsemen, perhaps in emulation of their Lydian neighbours.

Most of Greece, however, is not well suited to the rearing of horses and use of cavalry, and as horseshoes had not been invented, soldiers' mounts were apt to go lame in that stony country. This is attested by Xenophon,[2] who advocates the use of an expedient to harden horses' hoofs by inducing them to stamp on a pavement of cobblestones that matched the size of their hoofs. But here his inventiveness stops. Horseshoes have, in fact, been found in northern Italy which may go back to the early fourth century, but they are of Celtic provenance and so do not concern us here. On campaigns horses needed a deal of fodder and of water; and wars happened in the summer when water is scarce and horses are thirsty. Greek horses seem to have been everywhere on the small side. Big chargers were bred far outside of Greek lands, especially in Media, where there were wide plains and ample fodder and a native strain of exceptional size and strength.[3] In most Greek communities it was a sign of wealth and birth to keep a horse, and rich men imported racehorses from foreign parts. But, for the practical purposes of warfare, cavalry was nowhere the dominant arm south of Thessaly, where it maintained the rule of the local nobles over the half-serf population of its broad plains.

Cavalry had its uses for reconnaissance, though in a broken country even this was better done by light-armed infantry. When a phalanx broke in flight, horsemen were useful in pursuit; but, as has been observed, pursuit was not pressed far in early times. The flanks and rear of a phalanx were vulnerable to cavalry, which at times could immobilize or harry infantry. This happened when the mounted Thessalian allies of the Athenian tyrant Hippias worsted a smallish Spartan infantry force in the

---

[2] *Hipparch.* I, 16; *de Re equestri* IV, 3–4.
[3] See Pauly-Wissowa, *Realenc.* s.v. Pferd, cols. 1440 f.

plain behind the Bay of Phaleron.[4] And it happened again when, fifty years later, an Athenian invasion of Thessaly could achieve nothing against a mounted defence.[5] After the battle of Plataea, the Thessalian and Boeotian cavalry fighting on the Persian side delayed the victorious advance of the Greeks.[6] And before Syracuse the Sicilian cavalry did much the same against the Athenians in the first battle fought before the city.[7] When the Spartans operated in Asia Minor, their general, King Agesilaus, was at pains to raise some cavalry which enabled his army to face the Persian horse and to move securely in open country.[8] But, on the whole, Greek cavalry had few important successes to record until some way on in the fourth century.

This is not wholly a matter for surprise. There is a pleasing passage in the *Anabasis*,[9] in which Xenophon seeks to dispel his infantrymen's fear of the Persian cavalry by pointing out that ten thousand cavalry are only ten thousand men. "For no man," he says, "ever perished in battle from being bitten or kicked by a horse. The foot soldier can strike harder and with truer aim than the horseman, who is precariously poised on his steed, and as much afraid of falling off as he is afraid of the enemy." The one advantage he allows to cavalry is that it can take to flight with a better hope of survival. This ingenious plea was successful for its immediate purpose.

Now the chief fact that underlies Xenophon's picture of the precariously poised trooper is that the Greeks had not invented stirrups or the solid saddle to which stirrups are attached. This invention, which seems so obvious to us now, was, indeed, not made until the Roman Empire, when stirrups are first used by

---

[4] Herod. V, 63.
[5] Thuc. I, 111, 1.
[6] Herod. IX, 68.
[7] Thuc. VI, 70, 3.
[8] Xen. *Hell.* III, 4, 15.
[9] *Anab.* II, 2, 18–19.

nomads who practically lived in the saddle.[10] One can deduce
from Xenophon's works on cavalry that, without stirrups,
horsemanship was a difficult art, that in rough country a horse
and his rider were soon parted. Before the discovery was made,
a cavalryman could not have a firm enough seat to charge home
with his lance couched under his arm. Nor could he use the long,
heavy sabre, which is the trooper's best weapon against foot
soldiers. For if he missed his target he would fall off his horse
like the two Knights in *Alice Through the Looking Glass.*

In modern warfare, fire power has eliminated cavalry, which
no longer takes the field even to serve the purpose attributed to
it by the legendary Colonel in the Cavalry Club—the purpose,
I mean, of giving a touch of distinction to what would otherwise
be only a vulgar brawl. In antiquity, fire power was not the chief
danger: the chief danger to cavalry lay in steady and courageous
unbroken spearmen. Horsemen might ride up to a line of
hoplites and thrust at them or throw their spears. But what followed was a moment of extreme vulnerability as they wheeled
their horses away; or, if they stayed where they were, the thrusting spear of the enemy could reach the horse if it could not
reach the rider. And though the rider might wear a cuirass or
carry a small shield, the horse was not strong enough to be
armoured, as were the chargers of Parthian cataphracts or of
mediaeval knights.

The alternative was to ride straight at the enemy—to use
shock tactics—and the shock was almost as likely to unhorse
the rider as to overthrow his opponent. For cavalry to be at all
effective in shock tactics, the most skilful horsemanship was
needed together with most resolute and unflinching will to
advance. This combination was achieved by the Companion
cavalry of Alexander and by some of the heavy cavalry of his
Successors in the Hellenistic period. But, even so, if the attack

---

[10] For the evidence for the first appearances of stirrups see Tarn, *op. cit.* p. 75 n. 1.

was to succeed, it must be helped by a gap or weak place in the enemy line, or it must be directed against troops less well armed and prepared to resist a charge. To bring this about needed the coöperation of other arms, above all, of the Macedonian phalanx. Now and again before Alexander there had been clashes of horse in which cavalry in column had ridden over or through cavalry in a shallow formation.[11] In the same way, heavy cavalry could defeat lighter-armed cavalry unless these last were skilled in a kind of elastic defence and had room to evade a direct clash.[12] The Thessalian horse which appear on the defensive wing of Alexander's battle line were presumably trained in these tactics, as was the light cavalry of the Hellenistic period. In some armies, as in that of Thebes, light-armed infantry were, on occasion, interspersed with the cavalry, and this implies an open formation that was better suited to defence than to attack, and to skirmishing than a vigorous charge.

If cavalry did succeed in breaking its way through enemy infantry or cavalry, it required high discipline and firm leadership to make it halt at the right moment and re-form, as it would need to do if it was to achieve victory elsewhere in the field. "Nothing," wrote Marmont, "is rarer than the perfect cavalry general. The qualities required are of so varied a nature and are so rarely met with in the same person that they seem to be mutually antagonistic. There must be, first of all, a sure and ready *coup d'œil,* a rapid and energetic decision, which must not exclude prudence; for an error, a fault committed on commencing a movement is irreparable owing to the short time required for performing it."[13] These rare qualities Alexander possessed in an eminent degree. His greatness was shown by his swift decision when and where to strike,[14] his power of inspiring

---

[11] E.g. Xen. *Hell.* III, 4, 13–14, V, 2, 41.

[12] Diod. XIX, 29, 7; the word he uses is φυγομαχεῖν.

[13] *Modern Armies,* p. 31.

[14] In this he was superior to most of the Hellenistic generals, who were apt to commit their cavalry to the attack too early.

the Companions to charge right home, and his control of their movements when the charge had carried them through the enemy.

Alexander did more than show how cavalry might decide a battle; he showed, too, how it could make the battle itself decisive, by his relentless pursuit after Gaugamela. I will take leave to quote from Sir William Tarn: "Alexander's views of what constituted a victory were those of Nelson; men might drop and horses founder, but he kept up pursuit till dark, rested till midnight, started again, and never drew rein till he reached Arbela, 56 miles from the battlefield. He was determined that the enemy should never re-form as an army."[15] Battles were to be lost by victorious cavalry continuing its victory too far in the same straight line when it was needed elsewhere.[16] This error Alexander did not make, and his Successors only rarely made it. In most of the great battles of the Hellenistic period cavalry had the first and last word.[17] Marmont declared that a battle won without cavalry does not afford a decisive result. This, though never wholly true, was more nearly true after Alexander than ever before in Greek and Macedonian warfare.

To return to Marmont's aphorism.[18] When he says of a movement of cavalry, "owing to the short time required for performing it," he reveals what was true of cavalry, especially of light cavalry, in his own day, the time of the Napoleonic Wars. From Charles XII of Sweden onwards, cavalry had increasingly learnt to manoeuvre at high speed. Its great effectiveness in the battles of Frederick the Great was due to the fact that under Ziethen and Seydlitz his cavalry could achieve this. The moment for a decisive attack may be a fleeting moment, and the power of cavalry to seize it makes it an arm of especial promise. Both

---

[15] *C.A.H.* VI, p. 382.

[16] E.g. Ipsus; see Plutarch, *Demetrius* 29, 3.

[17] The great age of cavalry lasted for about a century after Alexander, and then the phalanx began to be the dominant arm. Tarn, *op. cit.* pp. 27 f.

[18] *Op. cit.* p. 32.

Alexander and the Successors made great use of light cavalry in battle; and the one cavalry general whom the Greek city-states produced before the military rise of Macedon, namely Pelopidas of Thebes, showed he could mount a cavalry attack with great speed. And though the Greeks and Macedonians had not the fine horses that were bred in the East, so that, for example, they may not have been so well mounted as Persian or Bactrian cavaliers, they may, for some purposes, have been all the more useful for that very reason. When control is all-important, there are compensations in not having aristocratic chargers that may take the bit between their teeth. That embodiment of cool common sense, the Duke of Wellington, when reminiscing to his friend Stanhope, made a comment that is not irrelevant in this context: "The French cavalry," he said, "are more often manageable and useful than the English, because it is always kept in hand, and may be stopped at the word of command. This partly results from our horses being better and kept in higher condition."[19]

So much for the horse and his rider, and now I will turn to a more majestic object, the elephant and his mahout. It is not inappropriate, for the appearance and trumpeting of elephants daunted all horses that were not specially trained to operate with or against them. I may add in passing that the appearance and smell of camels affected horses in the same way. Camels do now and then appear in ancient armies, and in the sixth century they discomfited the famous Lydian cavalry of Croesus.[20] But camels, though odious to view and endowed with the offensive spirit, did not enjoy the blessing of pachydermaty. And so—to return to elephants—elephants, in the early Hellenistic period, were chiefly used to neutralize the superior cavalry of an opponent; for example, at the battle of Ipsus in 301 a line of elephants was

---

[19] P. H. Stanhope, *Notes of Conversations with the Duke of Wellington, 1831–1851*, p. 221.
[20] Herod. I, 80.

interposed to prevent the possibility that the victorious cavalry of Demetrius would return to the battle.[21]

How Alexander himself would have used elephants we cannot say. He was only once seriously engaged with them, when they gave him a hard fight at the Hydaspes. The Persians had had fifteen of them at Gaugamela, but, for whatever reason, they do not figure in the battle. Alexander had well over a hundred of them on his return from his Indian expedition, but he never had an opportunity of using them in battle. Most of his Successors laid great store by them, especially Seleucus, who had fought against them at the Hydaspes and was to take the elephant as the badge of his dynasty.[22] Indeed, he ceded a large stretch of territory to the Indian king Chandragupta to obtain five hundred war elephants, most of which he used to great effect at the battle of Ipsus. Antigonus I made a great effort to surprise and capture the elephants of his opponent Eumenes of Cardia, but, well handled, they took care of themselves.[23] The Ptolemies founded a town called Ptolemais of the Beasts (Ptolemais Theron)[24] to be the base for the hunters sent out to capture these valuable quadrupeds. Some Hellenistic generals expended much ingenuity in making them live up to their reputations. They appear with light-armed troops, each affording protection to the other—or posted between the companies of a phalanx, so that the whole was compared to a wall with its towers. They are sometimes used as a screen for cavalry trained not to be frightened by them; and sometimes as a kind of advanced guard of infantry formations in order to break up or delay the enemy attack. In the battle of Paraitakene in 317, both the 114 elephants of Eumenes and the 65 elephants of Antigonus I were apparently to be used in this way, to judge from the order of battle given by Diodorus. But once the battle is joined nothing more is heard

[21] Plutarch, *Demetrius* 29.
[22] Tarn, *op. cit.* p. 94.
[23] Diod. XIX, 39.
[24] Or Epitheras; Strabo XVI, 768, 770.

of them, presumably from an oversight in Diodorus' copying out of his original sources.

On the other hand, in the battle of Gaza some five years later, Ptolemy, who had no elephants, held up those of his opponent Demetrius by using a movable arrangement of spikes connected by stakes and chains.[25] The elephants trod on the spikes with their tender and vulnerable feet. It was a device that had been used in Greece six years before in the defence of a town. The spikes would be felt before they were seen, and they provided, in short, a kind of antique minefield with the added merit of mobility.

Still, in that sophisticated age, when any new device was welcome, generals were slow to despair of elephants. They loom large through the mists of war; but they are not a talisman of victory. In fact, if all the battles in which they appear are examined, they are found more often involved in defeat than in the forefront of success. The seductive modern suggestion that they are the tanks of ancient warfare does them more than justice.[26] And it may be appropriate to observe that when skilfully assailed they may go into reverse, as in an attack on a Roman army in Sicily in the First Punic War.[27] And they were prone to panic and might trample down their own men, as at Magnesia. They were, indeed, chancy combatants and needed to be very skilfully controlled by their drivers. This fact underlines one ironical situation in which, after warlike exchanges, the elephants were found to be on one side and the mahouts on the other.[28]

---

[25] Diod. XIX, 83–84. It is a probable assumption that the barrier was of spikes as in the defence of Megalopolis in 318 (Diod. XVIII, 71, 2–6). Diodorus, writing of Paraitakene, speaks only of χάραξ σεσιδηρωμένος, but he may have misunderstood his source, as it is hard to see how anything other than spikes can have been effective. See R. M. Geer in Loeb translation of Diodorus, Vol. X, pp. 60 f., and H. Delbrück, *Geschichte der Kriegskunst*, I³, p. 243.

[26] See Tarn, *op. cit.* p. 95. On the use of elephants in general see R. F. Glover, "The Tactical Handling of the Elephant," *Greece and Rome*, XVII, 1948, pp. 1–11.

[27] Polybius I, 40, 13. See also *Bellum Afric.* 27.

[28] G. T. Griffith, *The Mercenaries of the Hellenistic World*, pp. 214 f.

Now and then, elephants were used with effect against weak fortifications, such as palisades, and once, by the Spartan captain Xanthippus in the service of Carthage with very great effect against massed infantry of the line. But in most battles, apart from their tactical use against cavalry, they were as much like a broken reed as elephants can well be expected to be. Their most striking successes in infantry battles were against troops that had never seen them before, against the Gauls in the famous "Elephant Battle" of 275 B.C.,[29] and in the first victory of Pyrrhus over the Romans, whose ignorance of these animals is attested by their odd description of them as "Lucanian cows," and in that of Xanthippus which I have mentioned. As time went on they appear in this army or that. At Cynoscephalae in 197 B.C. the few elephants in the Roman army may have induced a disastrous delay in the deployment of the Macedonian phalanx. Caesar went out of his way to train his troops to attack the elephants of the Numidian king, Juba.[30] When the Emperor Claudius appeared in Britain to lend the prestige of his presence to a victory already won, he added to his dignity that of some elephants. Thereafter they disappear from the scene of war; and after giving them due credit for their occasional successes, we cannot assert with confidence that, from first to last, elephants pulled their weight.

SIEGECRAFT

Before we reach the end of the means of warfare, we must arrive at the defences of cities, fortresses, or military positions and the means of overcoming them. By a slight misuse of language we may include both defence and attack in the one word—siege-craft. The archaeological remains of the Heroic Age in Greece reveal a few smallish fortresses of great strength and complexity as at Tiryns, which are the counterpart of mediaeval castles

---

[29] Lucian, *Zeuxis* 8–11.
[30] *Bellum Afric.* 72.

rather than of fortified cities.[31] But when the *polis* has ceased to be the citadel or place of refuge, and has become the republican city-state, fortification protects the heart of the community, its urban centre, and not merely the king and his immediate *entourage*. The city wall embraces an area in which a considerable part of the citizens can live in lasting security. The wall, usually of brick on a stone foundation, is not very high or very strong, for it does not yet need to be, though some attempt is made to give protection to the city gates. In Asia Minor some stronger fortifications are attested by the results of excavation, though in the middle of the sixth century these could not defeat the siegecraft which the Persians had learned from the Assyrians. But in Greece itself the walls of cities, simple as they were, sufficed for their purpose.

In historic Greece down to the first phase of the Peloponnesian War there is no certain record of a Greek city being stormed by Greeks. What cities had to fear was reduction by starvation or their betrayal to the enemy. Pericles is credited with the use of siege devices against Samos,[32] but as the city held out for eight months and then capitulated,[33] we may suppose it was reduced by blockade, by starvation or the fear of starvation, rather than by direct attack. In the Peloponnesian War, the small town of Plataea, after ingenious attacks which seem to have been regarded as the acme of contemporary siegecraft, was, in the end, left to fall to the long-drawn pressure of starvation after two years of close-drawn circumvallation.[34] The Athenians had some reputation for siegecraft, but Potidaea held out against them for nearly three years and then surrendered only on terms, and that too although it was important for Athenian prestige to bring the siege to an end as quickly and decisively as possible.[35]

---

[31] See Pauly-Wissowa, *Realenc.* s.v. Kriegskunst, col. 1829.

[32] Plutarch, *Pericles* 27.

[33] Thuc. I, 117, 3.

[34] Thuc. III, 52.

[35] Thuc. II, 70.

Sieges were very expensive: that of Potidaea was a great drain on Athenian finance.[36] When Mytilene revolted against Athens the city could not be taken until the beginning of starvation led to its surrender, when the mass of the citizens were armed and were able to get their way against the more determined aristocrats who had been responsible for bringing out the revolt.[37] So too the Athenians had no hope of taking Syracuse except by circumvallation or a movement for surrender within the city itself. The Long Walls at Megara were captured by a kind of *coup de main*,[38] helped by treachery; and Brasidas captured a few small places in Chalcidice. The hastily constructed defences of Delium fell to fire propelled through a kind of gigantic blowpipe; they were, however, no more than palisades.[39] But it remains true that until the last decade of the fifth century no Greek city of any size was taken by assault. Then in Sicily strong Greek cities were taken by the Carthaginians with engines of war and storming parties of barbarian mercenaries. This is the exception that proves the rule, as the rule is that Greek states would not face heavy losses among their citizens in what was then bound to be the hazardous adventure of an assault.

With the fourth century there comes a change. The invention of the torsion catapult and variants upon it added to the chances of assaulting cities.[40] It became possible to provide a longer-range, more intensive barrage which would keep down the heads of the besieged at the moment of assault, and break down the parapets which sheltered them. This fire might be directed from the ground or from siege towers. The fear of heavy losses in the attack, which had so long haunted Greek armies, was at least

[36] It cost 2,000 talents. Thuc. II, 70, 2. The siege of Samos had cost over 1,400 talents. Tod, *Greek Hist. Inscr.* 50.
[37] Thuc. III, 27–28.
[38] Thuc. IV, 66–68.
[39] Thuc. IV, 100.
[40] For details of torsion engines of war see E. Schramm in J. Kromayer–G. Veith, *Heerwesen und Kriegführung der Griechen und Römer,* pp. 220 ff.; Tarn, *op. cit.* pp. 103 ff.

reduced. It became easier to cover sapping and mining and the advance of battering rams of ever greater power. Cities went on fortifying their gates more and more elaborately, but their curtain walls were becoming more and more vulnerable, though the use of slightly projecting towers made it easier to enfilade the attackers than was possible with the simpler walls of the fifth century. But in the first half of the fourth century the full effect of siege engines was not realized, if one may judge from the contemporary book of Aeneas Tacticus on the art of defending cities, despite the brilliant attack on the strong place of Motya in Sicily by Dionysius I.[41]

Nonetheless, by about the middle of the century a kind of balance had been reached between attack and defence, and Philip II of Macedon with the new siege engines and the services of Greek engineers failed to capture the two cities of Perinthus and Byzantium. Then Alexander the Great revealed himself as a master of siegecraft. He pressed his sieges home with fiery and resourceful determination. No city however strong, and no fort however defended by art and nature, foiled his skilful attack, and if this had not been so, he could never have conquered the Persian Empire.[42] But what marked him out was precisely this determination backed by troops who never failed him in courage and patience. When the Greeks rose against Macedon after his death, they had not the ardour to storm the all-important fortress of Lamia,[43] and, later, Demetrius, for all the elaborate siegecraft that gave him his name of the Besieger, was baffled by the stubborn and resourceful defence of the Rhodians in the most famous siege of antiquity.

The art of defence had caught up with the art of attack. In the later fortifications of this century and the next, catapults of various kinds are used to keep at distance the siege engines of the

[41] Diod. XIV, 47–53.
[42] See Delbrück, *op. cit.* p. 175.
[43] Tarn, *op. cit.* p. 47.

enemy and cover with their fire ditches which would hinder the advance of the artillery and battering rams and siege towers of the assailants. By calculations which have survived in Greek writers, the calibration required for the discharge of missiles of differing weight to carry differing distances was scientifically determined. There have also survived in these writers the designs for engines of war, for stone-throwing and arrow-firing catapults and even a kind of quick-firing weapon. It was a challenge to Greek ingenuity which was triumphantly met in the course of the third century. And in more varied ways the defence of Syracuse against the Romans in the Second Punic War displayed the practical resourcefulness of the philosopher Archimedes.[44]

The performance of these torsion catapults and their kind obviously added to the efficacy of missile weapons.[45] The arrow-shooting catapult could hit a single man at 100 yards and a group of men at twice the distance. It was possible by using a high trajectory up to 45 degrees to reach 500 yards, but it was inaccurate at that extreme range. It could be used, as it was by Alexander, to fire across a river which was too broad for the range of archers and slingers. A stone-throwing catapult was effective up to 200 yards with the heaviest stone projectile they could discharge with an approach to precision. The catapults could outrange all nonmechanical missile weapons. But the power of their springing, which was usually due to the tensile properties of ropes of hair, quickly became lowered, and they took too much time for restringing to be really effective in warfare except as siege engines both in attack and defence.[46] And it is to be remembered that, useful as these were to keep down losses, what really destroyed the defences of cities was the battering ram, the sap, and the mine, or the tall siege towers,

[44] Polybius VIII, 5–6; Plutarch, *Marcellus* 15.

[45] The ranges are from Schramm *loc. cit.* above.

[46] This is the rule: a most notable exception is the use of catapults by Machanidas in the battle of Mantinea (207 B.C.); see Polybius XI, 11–12.

all of which were originally at home in the ancient Oriental monarchies.

All this competition of ingenuity in attack and defence did not cause campaigns to become a war of sieges as they became in Europe in the seventeenth century. The enterprising Hellenistic generals looked for quicker ways to victory. There were few points at which an impregnable city could greatly affect the course of campaigns. Strong positions might support strategic plans as did the great fortified *places d'armes* that were made by some of Alexander's Successors.[47] And they might strengthen political control like the three fortresses of Demetrias, Chalcis, and the Acrocorinth which were called the Fetters of Greece and were a mainstay of Macedonian predominance in the third century.

But the importance for my theme of these devices for attack and defence lies less in their direct effect than in the evidence they provide for the application of Greek ingenuity and Macedonian determination to the art of war. And while I am on this topic I may perhaps adduce some other instances of their military inventiveness.[48] When one reflects on modern inventions, it appears that most of them are only possible because of materials which were beyond the reach of the Greeks and Macedonians, such as india rubber, or of processes requiring more heat than they had the means of producing. They, or their neighbours in the Caucasus, were skilful metalworkers, but high-speed steel was beyond their power to make. They might rub a piece of amber and observe its reaction, but though they called amber *electron* they had not the means to produce electricity. The secret of Greek fire was jealously guarded by the Byzantine Empire, but antiquity did not know the stimulus of a patent

---

[47] On the other hand, even in Hellenistic times, camps in the field do not appear to be so well organized and fortified as they were by the Romans. (Polybius VI, 42, cf. V, 20, 4, XVIII, 18.) See A. Bauer, *Griech. Kriegsaltertümer*², p. 458.

[48] See, for most of these, Kromayer–Veith, *op. cit.* p. 243.

law which ensures the reward of the ingenious. The clear and nimble minds of the Greeks responded more readily to theoretical than to practical problems. But quite apart from the catapults—though even in these they were more fascinated by the problem of calibration than in the adaptation of materials—they did make inventions that served the purposes of war. For example, ladders; we find an improved scaling ladder to assist assaults and a ladder fitted with a shield to assist observation. Battering rams, as I have said, were made more and more powerful, and there was a device for boring into the foundations of walls, as there was an arrangement of bronze pans that recorded by their vibration the progress of a sap or mine. There was a kind of flame thrower and a forerunner of the Very pistol, and that without a knowledge of gunpowder. They applied vinegar to preserve a meat extract for the use of troops; the Maréchal de Saxe, who was devoted to the use of vinegar, quotes classical precedents for its beneficence. We find subterranean palisades or stakes to guard Mediterranean war harbours as was desirable in the almost complete absence of tides. The Greeks, like the Romans, did not fail to note the use of fire or smoke barrages to conceal or hinder the movements of troops.

If I had a more robust faith than I possess in the veracity of tradition, I could adduce the Messenians' story of their native hero Aristomenes that he floated down from a high cliff by using his shield as a parachute.[49] I would not think it proper to limit the acts of faith, and I would commend to consideration the account in Cornelius Nepos and Justin[50] of how Hannibal, when in command of a Hellenistic fleet, sent his sailors on shore to collect poisonous snakes alive. These he enclosed in fragile jars and propelled them into the enemy ships to spread

---

[49] Polyaenus II, 31, 2.

[50] Cornelius Nepos, *Hannibal* 10, 4–5, and 11, 5–6; Justin XXXII, 6–7. Justin speaks only of "snakes of all kinds," but this only slightly reduces the need for credulity.

abroad alarm and despondency, to match, I suppose, the uneasiness of mind of his own gallant mariners as they enlisted these ambiguous allies. The instinctive, perhaps pedestrian, reluctance that I feel to give wholehearted credence to this story does not remove my high regard for the unknown tactician who invented it and fathered it on Hannibal. And I have no serious doubt that this inventor was a Greek, and so I feel entitled to bring it within the ambit of these lectures. But for all I have said in this section, it remains true that the highest achievements of the Greek art of war are more to be found in the triumph of mind over mind than in the triumph of mind over matter.

V

The Means and Ends of Major Strategy

CLAUSEWITZ's famous definition of war as "a mere continuation of policy by other means"[1] is deceptively rational, for states may find themselves forced into wars which their policy never contemplated, which they would have avoided if they could do so without loss of honour or of freedom. So too when he defines strategy as "the theory of the use of combats for the object of the war,"[2] he narrows its scope too logically. Did not Napoleon say that a victory is always good for something? And states have been known not to look beyond victory in their strategy. Not all of them would have subscribed to the maxim on the plinth of General Sherman's statue in Washington, that the legitimate object of war is a more perfect peace. For my purpose it is at least more convenient to give strategy a wider range, though by saying major strategy I wish to exclude from treatment in this lecture strategy that shades into tactics, and to reserve that for generalship in battle. I include in strategy policies that must or may lead to war or may derive from it. And policy can be concerned with means and ends which may react upon each other. The policy of Great Britain in the nineteenth century pursued certain ends, usually defensive, within the reach of a large navy and a small army—though for a short period in the 'seventies what was called "jingoism" flattered

---

[1] *On War*, trans. Graham, I, p. 12.
[2] *Ibid*. p. 44.

itself by deducing policy from the doubtful proposition "we've got the ships, we've got the men, we've got the money too."

Let us turn from the jingo's song in the streets to the voice of Pericles or, if you will, the voice of Thucydides. He makes Pericles say on the eve of the Peloponnesian War that success in war is most often achieved by good judgment and abundance of money.[3] The word I have translated by "good judgment" means in this context "sound strategy," and "abundance of money" implies an already accumulated abundance or overplus. This dictum was applicable to the war Pericles proposed to conduct, but it is not everywhere applicable to wars between Greek states then or earlier. Very few Greek states had abundance of money, and some achieved successes in war without it. In fact, wars might begin with slight financial backing. A state's hoplites might appear with a few days' provisions and set off in a mood of faith.[4] While they were in the land of their friends, they were helped by their friends; and when they were in the land of their enemies, they helped themselves. They did not need many supplies, nor large stocks of ammunition. A modest train of vehicles or pack animals could usually serve their purpose, and though troops might be given pay for campaigning, campaigns were apt to be short and at times when farmers could afford to leave their farms. Long-drawn operations like a siege might need to be heavily financed, but sieges were rare. Thus the strategy of most city-states was not much limited by financial considerations.

But Periclean Athens was not like most city-states. She had a large fleet to maintain, and fleets cost money, for her oarsmen were often poor Athenians or rowers from her Empire who served for pay. To keep a single trireme in commission for a month cost a small fortune in terms of Greek money. Syracuse,

---

[3] II, 13, 2. τὰ δὲ πολλὰ τοῦ πολέμου γνώμῃ καὶ χρημάτων περιουσίᾳ κρατεῖσθαι.

[4] For Greek commissariat see K. Tänzer, *Das Verpflegungswesen der griechischen Heere bis auf Alexander den Grossen*. Diss. Jena, 1912.

Corcyra, and Corinth, which were well-to-do states, could keep up fleets of some size, and so could a few large islands in the Aegean. When the Corinthians hoped they and their friends could raise a fleet to challenge Athens, they had to hope, vainly it would seem, to draw upon the treasures laid up in the sanctuaries of Delphi or Olympia. Besides maintaining a fleet Athens had to be prepared to besiege cities, and several expeditions went overseas in order to maintain her Empire or injure her enemies. The early strategy of Pericles did require large financial reserves, which Athens possessed, and so for a time the means were available and were freely spent. More money was raised in the form of tribute, and the Athenians imposed on themselves, for a few years, a levy for the war, so that the annual drain on her accumulated treasures was reduced to about a third of what it had been.[5] Even so, it is reasonable to suppose that the running down of her reserves was one strong reason why Athens came to make the Peace that ended the first ten years of the war. When her reserves had been built up again during five years of comparative peace they made possible the Sicilian Expedition, which again was very costly. For the time of the last ten years of the war there is not much evidence, but there are signs that Athens was finding it very hard to pay her way. On the other hand, the financial weakness of her Peloponnesian enemies was remedied in the end by the aid of Persian subsidies.

In the fourth century the strategy of Greek states was often conditioned by financial need. Fleets were perforce smaller, and when Athens built up her naval strength again in the middle of the century it was a great strain which may have limited Athenian enterprise in other fields of war. In the war against the Persians in Asia Minor the Spartan generals, even Agesilaus, were tempted into faulty strategy by the wish to collect booty to finance their operations. In Greece itself the use of mercenaries prolonged wars in a way that was more to their

[5] Tod, *Greek Hist. Inscr.* 64.

advantage than to that of their employers. Because of financial stringency at the time of the Second Athenian Confederacy, Athenians were sent on expeditions which had to find money at the price of losing friends. With their more ample funds the Persian king or his satraps competed with Greek cities in the employment of some of their generals and some of their men. While the citizens would still come out and fight for their cities at the crisis of a war,[6] it was hard for the Greek city-states to keep them continually in the field. When Demosthenes proposed a plan for a standing expeditionary force against Macedon, to be composed in part of mercenaries and in part of citizens, he had to support it by careful financial estimates.[7] The early strategy of Philip II was largely aimed at securing for his treasury a source of gold and silver. It was, in fact, an age in which finance often helped or hindered strategy, and Philip knew this well.

When Alexander embarked on his invasion of Persia he was in serious financial straits, and his future was not a gilt-edged proposition.[8] He needed immediate successes in Asia Minor, and that was one good reason why he took a real risk in his first battle, that of the Granicus. From then onwards the conquest of Persia more than paid its way, and the immense hoards of gold and silver which he was able to seize in the Great King's treasuries set a high standard of military expenditure which his Successors, with wide territories to draw upon, were able to support. The *corps d'élite* in their armies were highly paid and paid all the year round. Antigonus I carried round with him an amply filled war chest to secure the loyalty of his soldiers, and most of his rivals will have done the same.[9] For two or three

[6] G. T. Griffith, *The Mercenaries of the Hellenistic World*, p. 5.

[7] IV, 28.

[8] *C.A.H.* VI, p. 360.

[9] Diod. XX, 108. See Griffith, *op. cit.* pp. 45, 51 ff., and, on the financial maintenance of troops, *ibid.* chap. x, and M. Launey, *Recherches sur les armées hellénistiques*, II (= Bibl. des écoles franç. d'Athènes et de Rome, fasc. 169), pp. 724 ff.

decades sound strategy was indeed supported by abundance of money. But the strain on the resources of their realms went far to undermine their prosperity and the loyalty of their subjects. And so the power of the Greek monarchies declined, even though the loyalty of the Macedonians to the house of Antigonus endured until the defeat of its last king, Perseus, which was at least hastened by his reluctance to exhaust his treasury to buy military help in an expensive market. In estimating the effect of finance upon strategy we have to remember that war in antiquity, so far as it was a business, was a ready-money business. Rulers did not possess the Fortunatus Purse of a national debt, which enables modern states to spend today the wealth they may possess tomorrow. Thus in major strategy we often find a nice balance between means and ends, not always to the advantage of strategy.

We may now turn from the interaction of major strategy and finance to the interaction of major strategy and geography. The mainland of Greece has more than its share of physical geography and, partly as a consequence of this, more than its share of political geography, so that it is full of frontiers, many of them moderately defensible. Professor Gomme in the admirable Introduction to his *Historical Commentary on Thucydides*[10] has raised the pertinent question why Greek states in the sixth and fifth centuries had not devoted their military potential to frontier defence. A partial answer to this question—suggested in my first lecture—is that the defence of mountain frontiers is better entrusted to light-armed troops than to hoplites. And city-states preferred to trust to hoplites for their safety, while light-armed troops, for reasons not wholly military, were not trained enough to perform what is really a difficult task, requiring initiative and an active and informed direction of command. And it must be remembered that mountains often defend noth-

---

[10] *Book I*, pp. 10 ff.

ing but themselves. "It has long been debated," writes Jomini, "whether the possession of the mountains makes one master of the valleys or *vice versa.*"[11] In the fourth century, when the quality of light-armed troops was higher and mercenaries could be more continuously employed than citizen forces might endure to be, problems of frontier defence were in fact studied, often with success. Where the territory of a state was as mountainous as in Aetolia, the strategy which the Aetolians used against hoplites was to allow them to advance and then to attack them with light-armed troops when they were far from the terrain in which they could operate with advantage. The borders between Attica and her neighbours Boeotia and Megara were for a long time guarded by a string of small fortresses sited with considerable skill, which were hardly ever captured by assault. But the frontier forts of Attica had very little influence on the course of the Peloponnesian War.

In that war there appears a strategical device which exploits the approachability of enemy territory whether by sea or by land. It is the device called *epiteichismos,* which meant the fortification of some place or region to put pressure upon an enemy.[12] This idea was in the air when the prospects of that war were under discussion; and it was tried, chiefly by Athens, not always with success. I will illustrate it by two instances that did succeed. In the first stage of the war the enterprising Athenian general, Demosthenes, occupied a position on the west coast of the Peloponnesus, which led indirectly to the capture of a force of Spartans, and directly, and more permanently, to producing a place of secure refuge for Spartan helots who wished to escape from being Spartan serfs.[13] It was repaid in kind when the Peloponnesians, in the last phase of the war, established a

---

[11] *Précis de l'art de la guerre,* p. 333.

[12] See F. E. Adcock, "ΕΠΙΤΕΙΧΙΣΜΟΣ in the Archidamian War," *Class. Rev.* LXI, 1947, pp. 2 ff.; cf. also, for the fourth century, Demosthenes, IV, 5.

[13] Thuc. V, 14, 3.

strongpoint at Decelea almost within sight of Athens. To this strongpoint Athenian slaves, mostly we may suppose from the mining areas of the south of Attica, where slaves were not well treated, escaped in large numbers. And it had also the economic effect of blocking a useful route to Athens from Euboea and the military effect of keeping the troops of Athens continually on the alert.[14]

Of more continuous importance for strategy was the holding of certain passes, most notably the Pass of Thermopylae. Again and again Thermopylae was the scene of such attempts, and again and again the defence failed, for the pass could be turned, until, in the time of Justinian, it was made the centre of an organized defensive region large enough to eliminate this danger. Once, indeed, its prompt occupation by the Athenians and their allies checked the advance of Philip II,[15] but it is not clear that the king had a sufficient incentive at that moment to bring on a major conflict, by seeking to force or to turn the pass. On an earlier occasion he had said that he drew back like a ram, to butt harder another time. It was even more like him to withdraw and wait for an opportunity when he would not need to butt at all; and in due course the opportunity came.

Having dealt with a geographical setting in which strategy is concerned to prevent an advance, we may turn to one in which strategy is concerned to make an advance timely and secure. The interaction of geography with strategy takes a wide sweep with Alexander the Great and the Successors. Alexander's aim to conquer the immensity of the Persian Empire posed for him problems of space, and the rival aims of the Successors to unite or divide between them this immensity did the same for them. And as their several ends were to be achieved by war, strategy of the greatest geographical range was imposed upon them. Thus to take one instance, Alexander's decision to eliminate the

---

[14] Thuc. VII, 27; 28, 1; VIII, 69, 1.
[15] *C.A.H.* VI, p. 220.

Persian fleet by occupying the coasts on which it was based, and to annex Syria and Egypt before he advanced to meet Darius, reveals a strategic wariness and a geographical calculation. His conquest of the Persian Empire was a victory over distance as well as a series of victories, first over Darius and then over opponents who sought to make mountains and rivers their allies.

This side of Alexander's greatness inspired the Successors, generals trained as they were in that eminent school of war, his camp. They achieved the strategical combination of widely separated forces, and exemplified in their practice the orthodox doctrines of modern military thought, as that in a war on two fronts you should defend on one front and attack on the other.[16] For they had an enlightened appreciation of the limits within which the maxim that attack is the best defence is more than a half truth. They moved large armies over great distances, and timed their operations to serve their far-reaching purposes. One side of the foreign policy of the Ptolemies, the double use of Syria as the glacis for the defence of Egypt and as a means to build and maintain a fleet, shows a nice appreciation of natural resources and of geographical advantages.[17]

Strategy may also depend on man power.[18] The king in the Scriptures who sat down to think whether with ten thousand men he could meet the king who came against him with twenty thousand was a more cautious strategist than the jingo in the jingle I quoted at the beginning of this lecture. The strategy of Sparta in the fifth century was conditioned by the fact that a substantial part of her strength was always needed to keep the helots in their place.[19] By contrast, the fact that Athens with her navy could use effectively in war a large class of citizens who in

---

[16] W. W. Tarn, *Hellenistic Military and Naval Developments*, p. 39.

[17] See A. Koester in J. Kromayer–G. Veith, *Heerwesen und Kriegführung der Griechen und Römer*, pp. 196 f.

[18] It is to be remembered that, in general, the Greek city-state had not large enough forces to undertake the lasting military occupation of any large area of enemy territory.

[19] See G. Dickens, "The Growth of Spartan Policy," *Journ. Hell. Stud.* XXXII, 1912, pp. 1 ff.

many states were never mobilized, extended her strategy far overseas in the fifth century. States could add to their man power by alliances, and that the more easily because hoplite contingents could be readily added one to the other. To help out her man-power Sparta made the most durable of Greek alliances in what is called the Peloponnesian League, but this meant that she had, in return, to have a care for the interests of her allies and some-times be guided by their wishes. In the making and maintaining of alliances diplomacy was at home, and Sparta produced a long line of skilful diplomats who must be remembered, if we think, what the Greeks did not think, that Spartans were men without guile. Behind Spartan diplomacy could be detected the prestige of the Spartan army, but that army was so precious an instru-ment that one aim of Spartan diplomacy was to avoid using it. Strategy and diplomacy went hand in hand during the later stages of the Corinthian War as each side sought to reach a military position which would give diplomats the best chance of winning the peace without generals' having to win the war. The strategy and foreign policy of Philip of Macedon worked together to add to his manpower the valiant mountaineers on his borders and the cavalry of Thessaly. And they worked to-gether so far as possible to subtract from each other the forces of his present or possible opponents. This example was not lost sight of in the statecraft and strategy of the Hellenistic powers, which often aimed at controlling territory which could supply them with contingents or, more often, afford to them a recruit-ment area of valuable mercenaries.[20]

There was another side of strategy which finds a place in Greek warfare, and that is the mobilization of what is nowadays called a fifth column. It was sometimes true in the fifth century, and more often true in the fourth century, that the strife of factions within a state afforded its enemies a hope that they

[20] See Griffith, *op. cit.* pp. 44 ff., 254 ff.

would get help from what may be called the opposition. For when strife was bitter, Greek politicians or partizans might rather see their cities in the hands of an enemy than in the hands of their political opponents. For example, on the eve of the Peloponnesian War the Thebans found men in the border town of Plataea who were ready to admit Theban troops and make their city not the ally of Athens, a bridgehead into Boeotian territory, but the confederate of Thebes, a bridgehead into Attic territory. And for a strategic end they sent troops on an enterprise which nearly succeeded.[21] But such devices as these were not always unsuccessful. For example, a Spartan force in the fourth century found it easy to seize the citadel of Thebes with the help of a faction within the city.[22] The oscillation of Argos between a more aristocratic and a more democratic form of government in the years that followed the Peace of Nicias made Spartan strategy political as well as purely military. When Brasidas led his bold enterprise against Athenian power in the districts towards Thrace, he must have counted on anti-Athenian movements in those cities, and his calculations proved sound. When Greek cities were hard to take, the besiegers were apt to trust, and often with justice, to treachery or at least defeatism in a city they could not capture otherwise. In his book on the defence of cities Aeneas Tacticus seems almost as much preoccupied with dangers from within as with dangers from without.[23] The devices whereby Philip of Macedon preëmpted assistance within states he wished to conquer or to neutralize became almost proverbial and even attracted the notice of the poet Horace.[24] Alexander in his invasion of Asia Minor made a shrewd strategic use of political propaganda against pro-Persian tyrants or oligarchies. And in the wars of the Successors one side of strategy

---

[21] Thuc. II, 2–6.
[22] Xen. *Hell*. V, 2, 25 ff.
[23] See especially chaps. II, X–XI, XVII–XVIII, XXII.
[24] *Odes*, III, 16, 13–14.

was to support those communities whose attitude was favourable and weaken those whose attitude was the reverse, or, better still, to induce communities to change sides, thus counting too on a division; though more often the tendency was to pursue military strategy pure and simple and leave military success to have its natural effect on the hopes or fears of the Greek cities. But, even so, the Hellenistic Age knew the specialized form of liberation which confers freedom to join one side but not the other. This process was easier as warfare was more humanely limited to the conflict of armies; for these shrewd strategists did not need Polybius to teach them that war should not destroy the fruits of victory,[25] and they would have agreed with Talleyrand when he told Napoleon that nations ought to do to each other in peace the most good and, in war, the least possible harm.[26]

There was one advantage which the Successors shared with Philip and Alexander—they were not only their own chiefs of staff but their own foreign ministers. This advantage was rarely vouchsafed to those who had sought to guide the destinies of the Greek city-states. Aristocracy or oligarchy tended to mean that authority was passed around; democracy tended to mean that authority depended on persuading Assemblies and so might be divided between generals and persuasive, sometimes rival orators or demagoges. Monarchy at Sparta was limited in policy by the ephors, or policy might be divided between the two kings, equal and opposite. Generals in the field might fear to do more or less than a Council or Assembly expected of them, and the fear of failure might make them overrash or overtimid. What happened to the Athenian generals after the first smaller expedition to Sicily was a warning which was taken too much to heart by Nicias in the second and greater venture.[27]

The fourth century showed the difficulty of due coöperation

[25] XVIII, 3, 4–8; see Tarn. *op. cit.* p. 44.
[26] E. M. Earle, *Makers of Modern Strategy*, p. 33.
[27] Thuc. IV, 65, 3–4; VII, 14, 4.

between statesmen who were not soldiers and soldiers who were
not statesmen. There was no continuing direction of over-all
strategy such as the Roman Senate could exert. The belief that
the democracy could do no wrong meant that the leader of
today might be the scapegoat of tomorrow. And secrecy might
not survive open debates on military policy. He would be a
fortunate Greek general who could say with Frederick the Great
that if his nightcap knew his plans he would throw it into the
fire. And, finally, strategy might not dare to be farsighted.
Demosthenes made bold to tell the Athenians that they were like
barbarian boxers who did not ward off blows but clapped their
hands to the place where they were hit.[28] But nonetheless the
Greeks were very intelligent about war, as about almost anything, and in a crisis they often had the wits and the courage to
rise to the emergency. When the news came to Athens of the
destruction of their fleet at the end of the Peloponnesian War
the word was passed up from the Piraeus to the city, and that
night no man slept, but next morning they were busy getting
their defences in order.[29] It was bound to be in vain, but it was
not a moral collapse.

I have quoted the legend on General Sherman's statue that the
legitimate object of war is a more perfect peace. In the fourth
century there were moments when the Greek states had achieved
what they called a Common Peace which might enable them to
do without strategy, but as it was achieved by strategy it tended
to be used for strategy and to defeat its own object. And in the
Greek world there was not enough elbow room, and there had
been too much history: the possible surfaces of friction lay too
close together and memories were too vivid. Statesmen who
sought peace could not easily administer to their peoples the
health-giving draught of the waters of Lethe. And the margin
of strength and the stability of policy which most Greek states

[28] IV, 40.
[29] Xen. *Hell.* II, 2, 3-4.

possessed was not great enough to afford scope for calculated risks which may be a proper part of foreign policy and strategy alike. And, here as elsewhere, the danger to peace might come from its old enemy, the strong desire to take no risks to preserve it.

There is another field in which strategy and foreign policy may join hands in the achievement of a balance of power that combines a military basis with a political calculation. The Thirty Years' Truce in the fifth century balanced for a time the naval strength of Athens against the strength on land of Sparta and her allies, the belief that neither side could be sure of defeating the other. So too the rival ambitions of Alexander's Successors, despite the utmost strategic and diplomatic contrivances, led to the realization for a time that the three great kingdoms of Macedon, Syria, and Egypt must fall back on coexistence lest worse befall them.

Now to come nearer to warlike operations. Bearing in mind the orthodox distinction that the theatre of war is the province of strategy, as the field of battle is the province of tactics, I will now say something about strategy as an antecedent to combat. Xenophon writes, "Wise generalship consists in attacking where the enemy is weakest, even if the point be some way distant ... ,"[30] and adds later, "If you attack expecting to prevail, do it in full strength, because a surplus of victory never caused any conqueror one pang of remorse."[31] These remarks support the definition of strategy as the art of bringing most of the strength of an army to bear on the decisive point, except that the decisive point may not be, though it often is, the point where the enemy is weakest. Epaminondas' attack in the battle of Leuctra, which was described in the second lecture, is an instance of the exception. We may recall General Forrest's recipe for military success, "Git thar fust with the most men." In that

---

[30] *Hipparch.* 4, 4, 14.
[31] *Ibid.* 7, 11.

phrase the little word "thar" is not otiose: it means "where it matters." This is clearer in Greek and Macedonian tactics than strategy. Most ancient writers on warfare give more attention to battles than to the movements which led to them, so that it is not so easy to collect material that bears on strategy. Furthermore, Greek armies, in particular, were rarely large enough, or organized in sufficiently large units, to practise the modern art of marching separated before fighting united. Nor as a rule were there good roads enough to make this feasible. The so-called grand strategy of Napoleon, to pin down the enemy by fighting and at the same time to place a strong force across his communications, is very rarely exemplified in antiquity, partly because, in the conditions of ancient warfare, communications did not matter so much, and partly because generals were reluctant to divide their strength on the eve of battle. For this reason, too, the holding back of a powerful reserve force to be brought into play at a later, decisive, moment is very rare indeed in Greek warfare and rare in Macedonian strategy.

The strategical use of long forced marches, which appears in Roman warfare most clearly before the battle of the Metaurus, is limited by the need of conserving the energy of troops for combat and, possibly, by lack of march discipline and good roads. But it was not unknown. The most successful instance that comes to mind is the brilliant stroke of Philip II in the campaign that preceded the battle of Chaeronea.[32] By a combination of deception about his purposes, the most careful preparation in deep secrecy, and a rapid advance ending in attack delivered with crushing force, he destroyed the ten thousand mercenaries that held the extreme left of the Allies' extended defensive line that had thwarted him for so long. By this stroke he turned their position and was able to bring about the pitched battle he had been looking for. Perhaps more impressive was a march by

[32] N. G. L. Hammond, "The Two Battles of Chaeronea (338 B.C. and 86 B.C.)," *Klio*, XXXI, 1938, pp. 186 ff.

Antigonus I.[33] In the year 319 he decided to attack a potential enemy, Alcetas, who was peacefully encamped nearly three hundred miles away with an army of about twenty thousand men. In a forced march of seven days and nights Antigonus moved his whole army, horse, foot, and elephants, all that distance, and fell upon his unsuspecting victim to his utter destruction. This means that Antigonus marched some fifty thousand men at a speed of some forty miles in each twenty-four hours. Such a feat would seem incredible were it not that in this period an accurate record was kept of each day's march by officers appointed for the purpose, and these records would be available to the ultimate source of the ancient account in the historian Diodorus. Two years later Antigonus tried his luck again.[34] He set out in the depth of winter to swoop down upon the army of his opponent Eumenes of Cardia, as it was hibernating nine days' march away in its camps and billets. The enterprise failed because Antigonus' army, though it would march with the best, after five nights of cold disobeyed the order against lighting campfires at night, so that the glare in the sky warned the enemy just in time. Had this second enterprise succeeded it would have established Antigonus' reputation forever.

What is nowadays called a pincers movement, the synchronized convergence of two or more armies, combined with surprise of the enemy, was attempted several times in the fifth century; once it came very near to success, otherwise it failed.[35] The combination of speed, secrecy, and, more especially, an exact calculation of time in the absence of rapid intercommunication, meant that conceptions which in themselves were bold and imaginative were too much at the mercy of mischance.

From major strategy before combat we may now turn to major strategy after combat. As was said in the first lecture,

---

[33] Diod. XVIII, 44–45.
[34] Diod. XIX, 37; Cornelius Nepos, *Eumenes* 8; Plutarch, *Eumenes* 15, 3–4.
[35] *C.A.H.* V, pp. 227, 229, 239 f., 269 f.

pursuit after victory in a hoplite battle was not prolonged, and early strategy did not seek to continue victory to the utter destruction of the opposing army. What has been called the strategy of overthrow went beyond the normal purposes of a city-state at war. But in this, as in battle tactics, we may attribute to Epaminondas the beginning of a new era in Greek warfare. The military predominance of Sparta had rested on an invincible army and what had seemed to be an inviolable country. Now, after destroying Spartan invincibility at the battle of Leuctra, Epaminondas in the winter of the next year marched down the Peloponnese, into Laconia, freed Messenia, which was half the economic basis of Spartan strength, and brought about the federal unity of Arcadia to be a counterpoise to Spartan power in the central Peloponnese. It was, despite the time that elapsed since the battle of Leuctra, a species of pursuit, not tactical for the battlefield, but designed to serve a long-range strategy and policy. In this it was, in essence, an action of the quality, if not of the scale and range, of the strategic pursuit after Jena that carried the French arms to the Baltic, or the strategic pursuit after the battle of Normandy that carried the Allied armies to the Rhine. Its rival was the strategic pursuit by Alexander of King Darius as an extension of the tactical pursuit after the battle of Gaugamela. Herein we find the means of strategy stretched to the utmost to achieve its most far-reaching purposes.

But strategy may not only aim at reaching combat at an advantage or profiting fully from victory. It may have the purpose of postponing battle or even of avoiding it as the direct way to a final decision. Here too a strategist may come into his own. When Marius was on the defensive in the first campaign of the war between Rome and her Italian allies, the opposing commander—doubtless an old comrade of earlier wars—cried out to him: "If you are a great general, come down and fight it out." And Marius replied: "And if you are a great general, make me fight it out against my will."[36] To find an instance of the skilful postponement of combat we may revert to Antigonus' attempts to surprise Eumenes of Cardia. When the distant glare of campfires against the night sky warned the nearest villages of the approach of Antigonus, swift dromedaries carried the news to Eumenes. His forces, largely despite his better judgment, were widely scattered, and if he was to fight a battle he needed a few days to concentrate his army. He used the few troops he had with him to mark out an area with a perimeter of some eight miles on high ground visible to the approaching enemy at a great distance. On this perimeter fires were lit about thirty feet apart. The men who tended these fires made them burn brightly in the first watch of the night, more dimly in the second, and in the third put out all but a few of them. Thus Eumenes contrived the appearance of a great army concentrated in preparation for battle with all the regular procedure of cooking supper, going to bed, and leaving a few watchfires for the pickets on guard. Antigonus almost inevitably deduced that his surprise had failed, checked his advance, and rested his troops against the day of battle, instead of marching straight on and overwhelming part at least of Eumenes' army and capturing part of his supplies.[37]

Besides the postponement of combat, there is a place for strategy aimed at avoiding it, though, as was said after Dunkirk, wars are not won by evacuations, and, it may be added, are rarely won without battles. Let me return to the dictum of Pericles with which I began. He speaks of "good judgment," meaning sound strategy. When he led Athens into the Peloponnesian War, his land strategy aimed at avoiding a pitched battle which Athens was bound to lose, and this though it meant the evacuation of the whole countryside of Attica. His

---

[36] Plutarch, *Marius* 33, 4.

[37] Diod. XIX, 38; Cornelius Nepos, *Eumenes* 9; Plutarch, *Eumenes* 15, 4–7.

object was to wear down the determination of the enemy. This
is what has been called the strategy of exhaustion or attrition
as contrasted with the Napoleonic strategy of overthrow.[88] It
does not deserve the contempt which has been lavished upon
it. Nor need it be entirely passive. It may indeed, as in the
classic instance of the Seven Years' War, lead to battles, but not
to a decision by battle. Pericles did not forgo minor operations
to harry and harm the enemy, and he would, of course, have
welcomed a great naval battle if his adversaries had dared to
risk one against an overwhelming fleet. So long as he lived and
controlled policy, he succeeded in maintaining this strategy.
And, apart from one single engagement on no great scale,
Athens adhered to this part of his plan. In the end, after ten
years of war, Athens secured a peace that gave her no less, if no
more, than what Pericles set out to attain. What he could not
foresee was the disaster of the Great Plague, which, by weaken-
ing Athens, postponed the day when her enemies admitted that
her strength was beyond their power to break. And he could
not foresee that his ward, Alcibiades, would induce Athens to
throw away the advantages of a Periclean peace.

[88] See H. Delbrück, *Die Strategie des Perikles erläutert durch die Strategie Friedrichs des Grossen.*

VI

Generalship in Battle

As THERE was such a thing as the development of strategy from the simple days of the hoplite phalanx, when military operations tended to be a walking tour ending in a combat, to the far-reaching and complex movements of the Hellenistic Age, so there was a parallel development of generalship in battles.

The ancient sources provide better evidence for tactics than for strategy, for most historians believed, sometimes rightly, that they could describe a battle, but few Greek writers except Thucydides, Xenophon, Polybius, and Arrian set out to describe a campaign. And some ancient authors, despite vaguenesses about distances and the points of the compass, have enabled us to know or reasonably conjecture where a battle was fought, so that we can go to look at the scene for ourselves.[1] It has, however, been my own experience that, wherever the face of nature could be altered by the shifting of rivers, the changes in coastline, or the level of a lake, the obliteration of a town or village, a malignant Providence has striven to deceive the observer. Only too often, despite much devoted and skilful labour by acute and careful scholars, the study of battlefields on the spot has been more warming to the imagination than illuminating to the mind.

The easiest criterion of generals in battle is the degree of their

---

[1] See especially for the geographical setting of battles J. Kromayer–G. Veith, *Schlachten-Atlas zur antiken Kriegsgeschichte*, and J. Kromayer, *Antike Schlachtfelder*.

success. As Machiavelli says in his *Art of War,* "If a general wins a battle, it cancels all other errors and miscarriages."[2] Drawn battles are rare, so most battles should make *one* general more eminent than he was before. But there is such a thing as a lucky victory, and there is such a thing as a soldiers' battle, to which a general has contributed nothing, or less than nothing. To be a good general it is not enough to be experienced. "A mule," said Frederick the Great, "may have made twenty campaigns under Prince Eugène and not be a better tactician for all that." It is not even sufficient to be old, nor, I may perhaps add, to be young. And to be a great general in battle is not just a matter of technique and applied intelligence. It has been well said: "Alexander, Hannibal, Scipio, Caesar possessed the highest faculties of mind. The same is true of the great Condé, of Luxembourg, the great Eugène, Frederic, and Napoleon. But all these illustrious men, while endowed with supreme intellect, possessed character in a still greater degree."[3] And to this list I would add Gustavus Adolphus and Robert E. Lee.

One side of generalship is the inspiring of confidence, and what soldiers admire is no one's business but theirs. The poet Archilochus does not conceal his preferences: "I have no liking for a tall or long-shanked general, nor one proud of his hair, nor one with shaven lip. Give me a man who is short and bandy-legged, firm set on his feet, full of heart and courage."[4] In the Peninsular War the Light Division said of Wellington that the sight of his long nose was worth a thousand men. In his African campaign Caesar's cheerfulness—his *hilaritas*—steadied his legionaries as they watched for the transports bringing much-needed supplies;[5] at Blenheim the unshakable serenity of Marlborough was able, if we may believe Addison, to ride in the

---

[2] *Arte della guerra,* p. 275.
[3] Marmont, *Modern Armies,* p. 188.
[4] Frag. 60 Diehl[3].
[5] *Bellum Afric.* 10.

whirlwind and direct the storm.[6] But we are not so much concerned with the greatness of men as with the art of war, of which their greatness is an ingredient.

I have spoken, in earlier lectures, of the generalship of Miltiades, Pausanias, Epaminondas, and Philip II, as of the strategy of Cleomenes I, Themistocles, and Cimon, the nautical skill of Phormio, the handling of peltasts by Iphicrates, and cavalry by Pelopidas.[7] Demosthenes, the Athenian general, showed enterprise and insight, both strategical and tactical, in the whole affair of Pylos and Sphacteria. The Theban Pagondas, who won the one considerable land battle in the first decade of the Peloponnesian War, namely the battle of Delium, may not wholly deserve the praise he has received. I do not wish to be unjust to Pagondas, who had at least that strong desire to fight which goes a good way to make a good general. And so I may be allowed to discuss this battle.[8] A substantial part of the Athenian field army was on its way home after establishing a strongpoint at Delium just inside the Boeotian border. Pagondas with rather more than an equal force of Boeotian troops was able to intercept them, and insisted on doing so. This was good strategy, for it was important to show that Athenian hoplites could not march in and out of Boeotia unchallenged. Hippocrates, the Athenian general, had left behind at Delium part of his small force of cavalry and had no light-armed troops of military value. Pagondas had one thousand Boeotian cavalry, which was always pretty good. He could presumably have retired until he found a battleground to suit his cavalry. As it was, he barred the way of the Athenians at a point where, in the normal formation of eight deep, they could fight with their flanks protected by watercourses on either side, if he attacked at once. And as he did attack before the Athenian general had finished going

---

[6] *The Campaign*, l. 292.
[7] See the Index, under each name.
[8] See Thuc. IV, 90 ff.; Diod. XII, 69 f., adds little of value.

along his line addressing his troops, the moment of attack was of Pagondas' choosing. The Athenian line of hoplites in the normal depth had to meet the charge, in which the right wing of the Thebans was ranged twenty-five men deep, so that the remainder of the Boeotian infantry army was inferior in numbers to the Athenians opposed to them. The result was that the Thebans had the best of it and their Boeotian comrades the worst of it, and it was a nice question whether the Athenian advantage in one part of the battle would not compensate for their disadvantage in the other. The battle seems to have reached an equilibrium, if an unstable one. Pagondas then sent a force of cavalry to make a *détour* round a hill and come to the help of his left wing. This was a wise move, and, had the ground permitted it, this cavalry might have intervened with good effect. But it was not a good terrain for cavalry,[9] and it is at least doubtful if this would have happened. What did happen was that the victorious Athenian right wing saw the cavalry appear on the skyline, believed it was the advance guard of a new Boeotian army, and broke in panic, and the battle was over. The intelligent Athenian hoplites had put two and two together and made it five. Had they been unimaginative Boeotians they would perhaps have arrived at the answer four (or even possibly three), and continued the battle so as possibly to get a draw if not a win. It is hard to believe that Pagondas reckoned on producing this psychological effect on the Athenians, and it is possible to think that his generalship was better rewarded than it deserved to be. But it is only fair to repeat that the decision to fight, if not at that particular place, would have been right even if it had not resulted in a clear-cut victory, as in fact it did.

The Athenian general, Nicias, was a better soldier than the final disaster before Syracuse would indicate. Had he fallen in

---

[9] G. B. Grundy, *Thucydides and the History of His Age*, II, pp. 134 ff.

the first battle before the city, his reputation would have stood pretty high. His conduct of operations since his first appearance had shown an awareness of new tendencies in warfare. In his amphibious strategy, in his skilful use of war engines, in his appreciation of the effect of cavalry, in his use of a defensive reserve, he was in advance of his times.[10] It is a fair judgment of him that he was swift in action but slow to make up his mind. At least, when he knew what he had to do, he was shrewd in contriving it. But at his lamentable end, beset by vain hopes and vain fears, he was, like Pompey at Pharsalus in Caesar's phrase, "summae rei diffidens et tamen eventum exspectans."[11] The career of Brasidas the Spartan presents a long succession of resolute, at times vehement, feats of leadership, coupled with an adroit management of men and events. He seemed able to do more with fewer men than any other general in Greek history. His last exploit, the defeat of Cleon's army before Amphipolis, was a combination of surprise, a shrewd insight into the flagging morale of the Athenians, and the inspiration of his own part of the army to attack a superior force.[12] But his contribution to the art of war was limited to his opportunities and marked no significant advance on the traditional tactics of the day. Of other Spartan generals of the fifth century, Gylippus at Syracuse was a determined man with an un-Spartan readiness to adapt himself to his task, and Lysander in the Ionian War was an equally determined man, who could understand a Persian prince, and could seize a naval opportunity when he saw one. Dionysius I of Syracuse studied the art of using a combination of troops in battle, but his merits lay rather in organization, fortification, and siegecraft than in the winning of battles. The history of Sicily thereafter added little to the art of war despite the adventurous strategy of Agathocles

---

[10] See e.g. Thuc. III, 51, VI, 21, VI, 67, 1.
[11] *Bellum Civ.* III, 94, 6.
[12] Thuc. V, 8–10.

of Syracuse[18] and the fortunate victory of Timoleon at the river Crimisus.

"The fortunate victory of Timoleon." There is, though, something more to be said about that. I have spoken of the part character plays in generalship, and it may outweigh talent and technique. The whole career of Timoleon was a triumph of character, perhaps the highest to be found in the history of the Greek city-state. There is no evidence that reveals in him outstanding military skill. But he was a resolute man who could resourcefully inspire his soldiers, and could turn a chance omen to good account. When the Carthaginians invaded Sicily with a strong army that included their heavily armed *corps d'élite,* the Sacred Band of citizens, he boldly met them with his small force at the river Crimisus. If he was to fight, there was no better place, but it was, by any calculation of probabilities, a forlorn hope. It resulted in a brilliant and decisive victory that saved the cause of Hellenism in Sicily. And why? The fortune that favours the brave opened the heavens, and it rained in blinding streams. The river Crimisus—like "the river Kishon, that ancient river" in the Scriptures—rose in spate when part of the Carthaginian army had crossed. The Sacred Band in its heavy armour stuck helpless in the mud and was slaughtered by the Greek light-armed troops, who could not have withstood its charge on firm ground. And the whole bewildered army was routed.[14] It was a fortunate victory. Rain does not fall at the bidding of the best of generals, and the wisest weather prophet could not divine that the crossing of the Crimisus and the heavy rain would coincide. But it was, at least, the reward of courage. And, after all, as Napoleon said, "qui ne risque rien, n'attrappe rien"; and here the choice was between all and nothing.

I now turn back to the Spartan king, Agis, who won the first

---

[18] See *C.A.H.* VII, chap. xix.
[14] Diod. XVI, 79–80; Plutarch, *Timoleon* 25–28.

battle of Mantinea in 418 B.C., a battle which demonstrated the military primacy of Sparta. He had shown himself an enterprising strategist in the previous campaign, but he may then have expected too much from a concerted plan that depended on the precise coördination of three forces moving at night.[15] Now, in this battle, at the eleventh hour, he ordered a rearrangement of his line which may have been promising, but only if he could count on his orders being promptly obeyed. They were not; and the credit for his victory may perhaps belong to the fighting power of his troops.[16] It may be suggested that, all in all, his intellectual reach exceeded his grasp, that he was one of those generals who, in Napoleon's phrase, "saw too many things at once." But his action at Mantinea is noteworthy because it shows a variation from the set and immutable character that had clung to the hoplite battle. One of his successors, Agesilaus, carried this further when, in the battle of Coronea in 394, he manoeuvred within the framework of the battle itself, even though he could not hold the attack of the deep Theban column and so complete his victory.[17]

On the other hand, the battle of Corinth that preceded the battle of Coronea has been well described as "a typical encounter of the pre-scientific age of Greek warfare."[18] It was a demonstration of the traditional Spartan tactics that were described in the first lecture. But the art of war was being studied and applied. Not only had Sophists added to the duties of a commander the acquirement of a general education, and Socrates and Plato sketched the philosophic portrait of a man skilled in war,[19] but lesser men set up as experts in the use of

---

[15] *C.A.H.* V, pp. 269 f.

[16] W. J. Woodhouse, *King Agis of Sparta and His Campaign in Arkadia in 418 B.C.;* A. W. Gomme, *Essays in Greek History and Literature*, pp. 132 ff.

[17] *C.A.H.* VI, pp. 47 f.

[18] *Ibid.* p. 47.

[19] See especially in the *Laches;* see also G. T. Griffith, *The Mercenaries of the Hellenistic World*, pp. 5 f., and H. W. Parke, *Greek Mercenary Soldiers from the Earliest Times to the Battle of Ipsus*, p. 39 n. 2.

weapons and the practice of command. In the *Anabasis*,[20] Xenophon describes with a touch of malice a certain Coeratadas of Thebes, who travelled round the Greek world offering his services as a general to all takers. Xenophon himself was not only a good practical soldier, but studied the art of war and wrote upon it, with common sense in his small manuals and with a touch of fantasy in his *Cyropaedia*.

The progress that was made in generalship is most readily tested by the position of the general in battle. He is no longer the man whose place is in the front rank of the hoplite phalanx once battle is joined. At Chaeronea, Philip must have directed the measured retirement of his phalanx from outside its ranks, though he may have charged with it when it turned to the attack.[21] Of Alexander's place in battle at the head of the Companions I will speak presently, but in the Hellenistic Age generals were apt to be on the wings or even, it may be, behind them, so that they could move about the battlefield at need.[22] The full-scale active reserve, as distinguished from precautions to limit the effect of a reverse, is almost unknown in Greek and Macedonian practice,[23] but the ordering brain of the general could now make new dispositions as the course of a battle might require.

But to return to my main theme. The watershed between the older and the newer battle tactics lies in the career of Epaminondas. Epaminondas by his innovations had won his first great battle, Leuctra, before it began. At Mantinea, his second and his last, he showed even greater generalship in prefacing his crushing blow by parrying not unadroit attempts to counter it in advance.[24] And, as has been seen in an earlier lecture, Philip

---

[20] VII, 1, 33 and 40.

[21] See above, p. 27.

[22] See W. W. Tarn, *Hellenistic Military and Naval Developments*, pp. 30 f.

[23] See Griffith, *op. cit.* pp. 30 ff.

[24] Xen. *Hell.* VII, 5, 22 ff.; Diod. XV, 85–87. See, for Epaminondas' tactics in this battle, E. Lammert, "Die geschichtliche Entwicklung der griechischen Taktik," *Neue Jahrbücher*, III, 1899, p. 27.

was skilful enough to create for himself the tactical advantage that made victory certain at Chaeronea. But between these battles and those of his greater son there is something of the difference that there is between chequers (or draughts) and chess. And it may not be too fanciful to compare the cavalry attack which was the decisive stroke in Alexander's battles with the knight's move in the hands of a master.

Alexander's first victory, at the Granicus, was assisted by the faulty dispositions of the Persians, but it showed how brilliantly he could bring his army into action.[25] His last victory, at the Hydaspes, was an equally brilliant solution of the problem of crossing a wide river and circumventing the strategy and the elephants of an able opponent.[26] But Issus and Gaugamela provide the pattern of the Alexander battle in all its subtlety and resourcefulness. At Gaugamela, for example, we must assume an over-all plan which provided for defence where and when it was needed, and for a decisive stroke where and when it could be most effective, by which the opposing king was driven from the field. It is true that there was a moment in this battle when Alexander himself charged with the Companion cavalry, and the white wings on his helmet, like the white plume of Navarre at Ivry, headed them to victory. Only so should the deadly thrust go right home, but, as a careful study of the battle has shown,[27] he neither lost the control of his Companions nor wasted the nice calculation that brought the phalanx and the hypaspists to grip the enemy, so that the attack could be exploited to the full. And he kept himself free, at need, to go to the help of the hard-pressed defensive wing upon his left. The battle displays also the subtle interaction of his covering troops so that the forceful tactics of part of the enemy could not thwart his prime purposes.

[25] *C.A.H.* VI, pp. 361 f.
[26] *Ibid.* pp. 407 f.
[27] G. T. Griffith, "Alexander's Generalship at Gaugamela," *Journ. Hell. Stud.* LXVII, 1947, pp. 77 ff.

The varied capacities of Alexander's officers and their instinct for meeting emergencies in the course of his multifarious operations, as well as in his great battles, were all needed to achieve his conquests. They were not easy men to lead nor soft metal to mould. They had to understand what they were about and improvise without waiting for orders: they had to be given their heads and trusted not to lose them. And with all their ambition and toughness of purpose they had to be what Nelson's captains were said to have been, "a band of brothers." That phrase reflects a profitable parallel suggested to me by a friend.[28] When Nelson's fleet was once engaged there was little opportunity to make any but the most general signals; but the constant conferences which the Admiral held with his captains gave them an instinct for the tactics that expressed the clear flame of Nelson's thought, so that they could conform to them with, if need be, the comforting knowledge that no captain could do wrong who placed himself beside an enemy ship. And as Nelson's flagship was a school of war, so, we must suppose, was Alexander's tent.

I must now pass on to Hellenistic times. In the first lecture I cited the dictum of Mardonius that the Greeks seek out the smoothest ground for their battles, and this was, in general, true of pitched battles between hoplite armies, which needed such ground to fight as they were taught to fight. It became true again of most of the great pitched battles of the Hellenistic Age; but this was not because tactics were simple, but because they were complex. The coördination of troops of different kinds, heavy cavalry, light cavalry, the phalanx or kindred formations of infantry, peltasts, light-armed troops of this kind or that, with the frequent addition of elephants, was hardly possible except where the battlefield offered ample room. The armies were apt to be bigger, often far bigger, than the old

<hr />

[28] By Mr. Griffith.

hoplite armies.[29] The deployment of two such large bodies of men in a complex pattern needed to be carried out at a considerable distance from the point of conflict. Thus, before the battle of Gaza, Ptolemy and Seleucus had time to change the disposition of their forces when they discovered that Demetrius had placed his attacking strength on his left and not on his right, as generals had normally done since Alexander. Alexander at Issus and Gaugamela had advanced with his army in battle order and this had become the usual practice. Generals were able to plan how they would fight a battle, and their subordinate commanders could be instructed how to act so as to fit in with the plan, and possibly how they were to meet foreseeable hindrances to its success.

Almost all the moves and countermoves of Hellenistic generalship can be exemplified in the series of three battles, Paraitakene, Gabiene, and Gaza,[30] which were fought between generals trained in the school of Alexander (with the addition of the young Demetrius, versed from boyhood in the teachings of that school). All three battles were fought in plains, the chessboard, as it were, on which the diverse pieces were moved in attack and defence. Highly trained troops were led by highly trained officers. It was for the generals commanding a whole army or a large part of one to engage in a competition of wits and will of the utmost complexity. Chance could not be ruled out. At Gabiene the dust raised by manoeuvring cavalry produced the fog of war in which Antigonus could move to his design. It was for the general to seize every advantage chance and local success offered to him and so to offset, if he could, the advantages which they offered to his opponent. At Paraitakene, as Antigonus saw the invincible advance of the famous Silver

---

[29] For the size of the hoplite armies of the city-states see K. J. Beloch, "Griechische Aufgebote," *Klio*, V, 1905, pp. 341 ff., VI, 1906, pp. 34 ff.; for that of the armies of the Hellenistic Age, H. Delbrück, *Geschichte der Kriegskunst*, I³, p. 289.

[30] See Kromayer, "Drei Diadochenschlachten," in *Antike Schlachtfelder*, IV, pp. 391 ff.

Shields of Eumenes, he countered it by a flank attack elsewhere which brought it to a halt. Or, to take a later battle, when at Ipsus Demetrius' cavalry carried all before it on the right and he disappeared in a triumphant cloud of dust, disappeared, as it were, off the board, Seleucus moved his elephants to prevent his ever returning, and Antigonus' infantry was worn down and either deserted him or was defeated. The generals in all these battles exhibited the Macedonian art of war on the highest plane. Battles had been lost by victorious troops assailing an enemy's camp, but a battle was won when at Gabiene Antigonus took his chance and captured the possessions of the Silver Shields, which they ransomed by the surrender of their general, Eumenes, and desertion to his enemy. Antigonus accepted the victory, but he saw to it that the Silver Shields never fought in a great battle again.

The eminent military qualities of the Successors are not easy to assess, but if they were eminent in degree, they were diverse in quality. Antigonus was, it would seem, an enterprising general, who carried determination to the point of obstinacy and so, at times, overtaxed his troops. Eumenes of Cardia was a good leader of light cavalry and a man of rapid decision and almost infinite resource. His one defect, which he could not remedy, was that he was not a Macedonian and hence could not always get his way. The first Ptolemy seems to have had a cool capacity to foresee and counter dangers. The first Seleucus was perhaps the most farsighted strategist of them all, as appears from the campaign of 302 which preceded the battle of Ipsus in the next year.[31] Lysimachus was a master of the defensive with the rare power to win time by surrendering space. If Wellington's dictum is true, that the sign of a good general is to know when to retreat and how to do it, Lysimachus was one of the best.

In the next generation the most notable figure was Pyrrhus,

---

[31] See Tarn in *Class. Rev.* XL, 1926, pp. 14 f.

though he won battles rather than campaigns. He wrote about warfare and gave what mind he had to its study. For example, he seems to have realized the weakness of the phalanx of his day; that formation had by then lost its old flexibility. Thus he posted Italian companies in the line of his phalanx to give it just this quality.[82] He also guarded its vulnerable flanks with cavalry and elephants. But the Macedonian tradition was already becoming overformalized, and he may have failed to win the crucial battle of Beneventum by an overrefinement of manoeuvre in hilly country and at night. Encounter battles in such country were in fact more suited to Roman tactics and to the greater elasticity of the legions which Polybius was to emphasize in the next century. Philip V, for instance, though a good strategist with a notable instinct for speed and surprise—for "the swift sharp thrust carefully organized and delivered when and where it was least expected,"[83]—was defeated in an encounter battle at Cynoscephalae as was his son Perseus at Pydna. But in the second half of the third century Macedon and Greece produced notable soldiers, and the quality of three of them may be exemplified from the course of one single battle.

The battle of Sellasia was fought in the twenties of the third century.[84] Antigonus III, surnamed Doson, with an experienced army of all arms, was faced by Cleomenes III of Sparta with a weaker force in a strong defensive position. The key to the Spartan position was a hill, Euas, on its left. It was held in some strength and was steeper than one could expect troops to carry by assault against any serious resistance. If it was held, Cleomenes could pivot on it and, at need, have a way of retreat. On his right was a plateau which gave room for the deployment of his Spartan phalanx and in the centre a rather narrow valley

---

[82] Polybius XVIII, 28, 10; Tarn, *Hellenistic Military and Naval Developments*, p. 14.
[83] F. W. Walbank, *Philip V of Macedon*, p. 44.
[84] *C.A.H.* VII, pp. 760 ff.; Delbrück, *op. cit.* I², pp. 244 ff.; Kromayer, *Antike Schlachtfelder*, I, pp. 199 ff.

with a river running through it. For some days Antigonus Doson studied this formidable position and then decided to assail the hill Euas by a brusque attack with light-armed troops. The defenders let the attack get too far before they charged and the hill was taken. By this stroke Doson had not yet won the battle, but he had made certain that if he won it, it would be decisive. The retreat of the Spartan army was compromised and the Macedonian phalanx moved forward to the decisive clash on the plateau. So far Antigonus Doson's share in the battle.

Meanwhile another soldier had revealed his promise. Serving in the central valley with the allies of Doson was a young Greek officer, Philopoemen. As the attack on the hill was developing, the troops of Cleomenes in the centre began to take it in flank. The assault might be defeated, unless, as is possible, that part of it was a feint. But whether that was so or not, what the moment needed was action, and without orders or against orders Philopoemen led a charge that was wholly successful. And when complaint was made to Antigonus of this insubordinate act by a young man, the king smiled and said: "The young man has acted as a great general."

Finally, Cleomenes, though his position was turned by the capture of the hill Euas, did not try to draw off his army. Instead, he committed his own phalanx to an attack which, in the end, after hard fighting, failed because of the great weight and experience of the Macedonian phalanx. Its failure meant destruction, and Cleomenes, the first Spartan king to survive defeat, rode off to a ship that was waiting for him in the harbour of Gythium. The question is whether this attack was good generalship or bad. The answer seems to be that, with the hill Euas lost, he had no good line of retreat, and that the only thing that could save Sparta was a victory that day, for the remnant that might escape could offer no serious resistance in a war of manoeuvre and Sparta itself could not survive a siege. The attack had small chance of success, but a small chance was better than no chance at all. And in war there are times when "bad is the best," and a good general must challenge fate and not surrender to it. The conduct of the battle by Antigonus Doson is a model of perception and timing, the action of Philopoemen was the earnest of a career which made him the best general the Greek city-states produced after Epaminondas,[35] and the attack of Cleomenes places him in the ranks of generals whose reputation deserves to survive defeat.

By now the military strength of Rome was becoming apparent, and in a very few years the struggle between Hannibal and the Republic held the stage. The days of the great Hellenistic captains were over and the generalship of Philip V was to fail before the legions. It was, indeed, the good fortune of Rome that she did not have to match her generals against Alexander and his Successors. And it is not to be forgotten that, in her conflicts with Macedon and Seleucid Syria, Rome was assisted by Greek troops under Greek commanders. And one of the first of Rome's victories in the East was also the last victory won by the methods of Alexander the Great. At the battle of Magnesia, King Antiochus had carried out the typical Hellenistic flank attack with cavalry and had turned the left of the Roman army, when Eumenes of Pergamum, fighting on the Roman side, led a charge of horse which routed the left wing of Antiochus' army and then turned on its phalanx, which was gripped by the attack of the legions in the centre.[36] It was an Alexander battle with Eumenes of Pergamum in the role of Alexander, and he can claim to be not the least in the long line of Hellenistic cavalry generals.

---

[35] The mature skill in battle of Philopoemen is displayed in the battle of Mantinea (207 B.C.). For his study of the art of war and military reforms see Polybius X, 22–24, Livy XXXV, 28, 1–7, Plutarch, *Philopoemen* 4–5.

[36] See *C.A.H.* VIII, pp. 222 ff.; Kromayer, *Antike Schlachtfelder,* II, pp. 154 ff.

What I have sought to describe in these lectures is the varied contribution of Greeks and Macedonians to the art of war. It is varied not only in its methods, but in the degree of its success. That in the end, when the great days were over, it succumbed to the material force of Rome, to the adroit policy of the Senate which used Greeks against Macedonians, and to the disciplined steadiness of the legions, should not lead us to discount its achievements. The future development of war and the military art and practice was to owe far more to the Roman tradition than to the Greek or Macedonian. But in its day, and in its way, it is, I venture to think, an instructive chapter in the long history of the art of war, and it illustrates, above all, the mind of the Greeks and the will of the Macedonians.

Appendix

The Literary Sources

WHAT was said in the first lecture about the beginnings of Greek warfare in the city-state is, of necessity, based on reasonable deductions from Greek weapons, Greek institutions, Greek terrain, and so forth. When the earliest wars of historical Greece were happening, no one was writing their history. With the fifth century we may turn to Herodotus, who could have talked with veterans of the Persian Wars he describes and even, it may be, with Aeschylus, whose *Persae* is instinct with a lively memory of the battles in which he fought. But though Herodotus was many admirable things, he was not what Caesar says *he* was—a "military man." Greek warfare in Herodotus has an epic quality which does justice to the greatness, the moving character, of the events which he describes, but he contributes little to our understanding of the art of war. When we pass to the second half of the fifth century we do possess a contemporary historian of the very first rank, who did understand war. Thucydides describes it with a clear appreciation of what brought victory or defeat. He makes Pericles rationalize war though with the knowledge that there is in it an irrational element of chance. He believed that war demanded courage and resourcefulness, the flexibility of mind and clarity of thought that gave the best chance against chance. He strives to set forth the operations of war with a candid evaluation of the essentials of the situation so far as he could discover them.

In his generals' speeches before battle Thucydides is not so much concerned with their emotional appeal as with the factors which govern not the battle alone, but the essential character of war,[1] and at times the military quality of the general concerned. He is not prone to praise or blame: he does not make excuses, even for himself, nor does he judge only by success. When the Athenian soldier, Cleon, promised to capture the Spartans on Sphacteria in twenty days, Thucydides says it was a mad promise because it was one,[2] even though under Demosthenes' guidance it was fulfilled, and because Cleon made it, and Cleon was not a good general as other events were to show. Thucydides understood war, partly because he had experience of it, partly because he needed to understand to make his work useful to future generals in war as to future statesmen on policy. But while he does make clear the operations of the Peloponnesian War as he judged them, the economy of his work and the evidence at his disposal may deny to us details, such as of terrain, which might enable us to try to judge the precise course of events for ourselves. Professor Gomme[3] has made clear how Thucydides takes more knowledge for granted than we possess about the way wars were conducted by himself and other generals of his time. But it remains true that we understand the Greek wars of the last half of the fifth century better than we understand any other wars before the campaigns of Caesar.

When Thucydides' history ends and the story of the Peloponnesian War is taken up by Xenophon in his *Hellenica* the intellectual temperature falls. Xenophon's *Anabasis* is, within its range, a military document of great value. It is based on first-hand knowledge of events in which he took a leading part. He was an excellent practical soldier, and other of his works show how he reflected upon various sides of war. But in his *Hellenica*

---

[1] See O. Luschnat, "Die Feldherrnreden im Geschichtswerk des Thukydides," *Philologus*, Suppl. XXXIV, 2, 1942.

[2] IV, 39, 3.

[3] *Historical Commentary on Thucydides, Book I*, Introd.

he does not reveal the penetration or high impartiality of Thucydides. The rather later historian, Ephorus, was not a good military historian if we may judge from the reproduction of his work by Diodorus and the strictures of Polybius,[4] who however allows to him some understanding of naval warfare.

There is much to be learnt from what remains of Polybius either to be found in so much of his writings as has survived or preserved at second hand by Livy. Polybius, too, was a man of military experience who had access to good material and applied his mind to the art of war with rigour and sometimes self-righteousness. Finally, we have an account of the campaigns of Alexander the Great that is largely based on works written in the generation after Alexander's death. It is by Arrian, who also wrote on the art of war in his own day four hundred years later. He is not always easy to interpret, but it is due to the survival of his writings on Alexander that we can understand the greatest achievements of the greatest Macedonian master of war.

For the later exponents of the Greek and Macedonian art of war (as of Alexander himself) there is much good material to be found in those parts of Diodorus' *History* which are derived from contemporary sources; this is true also of the Greek *Lives* of Plutarch, as those of Eumenes of Cardia, Demetrius, Pyrrhus, and Philopoemen, and in his Roman *Lives* where generals of the Republic were facing Hellenistic commanders in the field.

In the limited field of the defence of cities there is something to be learned from the surviving book of Aeneas Tacticus written about 357 B.C.; but he looks backward to recent history rather than realizes the new developments in war that were going on. On some technical matters such as ballistics and fortifications there are some rather later writers, but they are more concerned with the making of engines of war and the building of walls to match them than with their use. The later writers on tactics like

---

[4] XII, 25.

Aelian, Arrian, and Asclepiodotus are apt to repeat each other and repeat the past and are more concerned with tactical movements in a vacuum than in actual warfare. Finally, there is a collection of stratagems hastily compiled by Polyaenus to illuminate the dim mind of Lucius Verus on his Parthian campaign. It is uncritical, as is its Roman counterpart, the work of Frontinus, but it is, at the worst, the sediment left behind by the tides of war. Nonetheless, if these sources of knowledge, the evidence of archaeology, and the actual scenes of battles are studied, it is a manageable task to reconstruct the general advance of Greek and Macedonian warfare until, in the end, it declined into a certain rigidity and formalism.

INDEX

Index

Achilles, 2
Acrocorinth, 61
Aegospotami, battle of, 37
Aelian, 102
Aeneas Tacticus, 59, 73; as source, 101
Aeschylus: *Agamemnon*, 9; *Persae*, 13, 33, 99
Aetolia, Demosthenes' campaign in mountainous, 17 f.
Aetolians, as light-armed troops, 17, 20
Agathocles, 86
Agesilaus, 23, 49, 66, 86
Agis I, 87
Agrippa, 40
Ajax, 2
Alalia, battle of, 32
Alcetas, 78
Alcibiades, 11, 81
Alexander the Great, 83; at Chaeronea, 27; Gaugamela, 90; Granicus, 90; Hydaspes, 90; Issus, 90; siegecraft of, 59; strategy of, 43, 46, 70 f.; use of cavalry, 50 ff.
Amphipolis, battle of, 86
Amphitryon, in Euripides' *Hercules Furens*, on archery, 15
Antigonus I, 43, 54, 67, 78 ff., 92 f.
Antigonus III, Doson, 94 ff.
Antimenides, 19
Antiochus the Great, 47, 96
Arcadia, 79; source of mercenaries, 20
Archers, 14 ff.; mounted, 47; arrows, range of, 15
Archilochus, cited, 10, 23, 83
Archimedes, defence of Syracuse, 60
Aristomenes, 62
Aristophanes, cited, 21
Aristotle, 2; cited, 24
Armies: hoplite, chap. i *passim;* standing, 4 n. 6
Arrian, as source, 101 f.
Artaxerxes II, 20
Artemisium, battle of, 32
Asclepiodotus, 102

Athens: as fortress with Piraeus, 17; finances, 66; food supply, 43; naval supplies, 45. *See also under* Fleets

Balance of power, 76
Barce, 47
Battering rams, 60
Beneventum, battle of, 94
Black Sea, 43
Blockade, 37, 45
Boarding in naval warfare, 30, 34, 39 f.
Boeotian cavalry, 47 ff., 84
Bolis the Cretan, 24
Bosporus, 43
Brasidas, 35, 73, 86
Byzantium, siege of, 44

Caesar, 56, 83, 100; cited, 86
Camels, 53 f.
Camps, Greek, 4 n. 8, 61 n. 47
Carthaginians, 58, 87
Cataphracts: warships, 39; Parthian horse, 50
Catapults (torsion), 58, 60; arrow firing, 60; stone-throwing, 60; calibration of, 60, 62; ranges of, 60
Cavalry, 47–53 *passim;* against hoplites, 14; Alexander's use of, 50 ff.; combined with light-armed troops, 18, 51; with phalanx, 51; distribution of, 47 f.; generals, 25, 51, 53, 86; heavy, 51, 91; light, 51 f., 91
Chabrias, 23
Chaeronea, battle of, 27, 44, 77, 89 f.
Chariots. *See* War chariots
Cimon: naval improvements of, 33; strategy of, 42 f.
Circumvallation, 57
Claudius, elephants of, 56
Clausewitz, cited, 64
Cleomenes I, 41
Cleomenes III, 94 ff.
Cleon, 86, 100
Coeratadas of Thebes, 89
Combined operations, 41, 78, 87

105